AF271784

God and Email

Real life encounters with God

God and email.

God and email
© 2008 Mark Craythorn

Contents

1. *God is in the small things.*

Then a great and powerful wind tore the mountains apart and shattered the rocks before the Lord, but the Lord was not in the wind. After the wind there was an earthquake, but the Lord was not in the earthquake. After the earthquake came a fire. But the Lord was not in the fire. And after the fire came a gentle whisper. When Elijah heard it he pulled his cloak over his face and went out and stood at the mouth of the cave. Then a voice said to him, "What are you doing here, Elijah".

Elijah knew deep inside himself that the gentle whisper had come from God and now here was this voice at the mouth of the cave confirming it. God himself, the very creator, was asking Elijah what he was doing. It was not as if God did not know what Elijah was doing but the voice served to call attention to Elijah, to stop him in his tracks, and make him question exactly what he was expecting from God. Elijah didn't get what he expected. He had expected great and powerful things to come from God but all he got was a whisper, a gentle voice from above. It was a whisper and a voice that transformed Elijah and it is the same whisper and voice that will transform you.

The purpose of this book is firstly to show you that you too can hear that whisper and that voice, and secondly to encourage you to speak to God, placing yourself in a position that will cause Him to speak back to you.

Before we get started on our journey you first you need to know that God still speaks clearly to people today. You see, if God is the same yesterday, today and tomorrow then when we read about God speaking to Biblical figures such as Moses, Adam, Joseph and Elijah many, many years ago, it should come as no surprise to find out that He continues to speak to people today. God doesn't change. What He has done for others He can do for you.

God and email.

Perhaps you didn't know that God is still in the business of speaking to people just like you? Perhaps you doubt that God could speak to you? Could it be that, possibly, no one has ever shown you how to listen to God's still small voice, or could it be that you don't take the time to slow your life down to a place where you can stop and listen for God's still small voice.

Perhaps God is speaking. Perhaps what is happening is that He is speaking to you and you are not hearing Him simply because you have tuned Him out, like one might turn a radio dial off the channel that it is broadcasting on. Perhaps to start hearing Him you simply need to get back on the correct channel.

Perhaps you are asking, why you don't see the evidence of God's presence in this world that you are expecting to see? I am suggesting that perhaps to start seeing His hand in your life you simply need to be looking in places other than the earthquake and the fire. You like Elijah may initially have been looking in the wrong place.

I am going to suggest to you that what you need to do is to pause for a while in your busyness. Stop what you are doing, speak to God and wait for a reply. The reply may be immediate or it may take a while but if you expect God to reply then God Himself will come to you and will speak to you when you least expect it.

William is a very real person, a pastor, living outside Boston. He bought a book and didn't stop for one minute to think that God could be interested in something as small and mundane as him buying a book. Yet God was interested, very interested, and God prompted me living miles away in Columbus Ohio to send William an email. This is what I wrote to him:

From: Mark Craythorn
[mailto:markcraythorn@hotmail.com]

> Sent: Saturday, February 18, 2006 11:48 AM
> To: William@xxxxxx.com
>
> William,
> Did you buy a book yesterday? The Lord is speaking to me about you and a book.
> Blessings
> ~Mark

Notice that William and I live almost 800 miles apart, and although we are friends we are not in the habit of emailing each other regularly. The point that I would like to emphasize is that I really had no idea what was going on in William's life that day. That is, until God got involved and told me what was going on in William's life. William replied:

> From: William@xxxxxx.com
> To: markcraythorn@hotmail.com
> Date: Sat, 18 Feb 2006 18:31:27 -0500
>
> I bought 4 books yesterday.
> Three are required for my preaching class.
> ….…..

William had indeed bought a book. Not only that but He had done it at the exact time I specified. If it were not for God, how would I have known about the purchase, that it was a book, or even when the purchase had taken place? William is a pastor, and God had just whispered to him.

William was so impressed that he mentioned the incident to a gathering of men from his church. A seemingly trivial matter of purchasing a book suddenly became infused with the sacred things of God.

Your life is infused with the same sacred things of God. Perhaps you are not even aware of it? Perhaps you doubt that God is interested in your life? Let me first assure you that God in fact delights in you and your life. He is intimately aware of and concerned with all that you are going through and He takes delight when you draw near to Him.

William had bought 4 books, and as he and I discussed this later on the phone, it turned out that one of the books was more significant than the others. As we will see later, hearing God is not an exact science; God is more interested in the relationship between Himself and us than He is in the science of the relationship. God wants to spend time with us and often does, breaking through into our lives at any time. If we are not careful we will miss these moments.

God also wants us to get excited about what it means to have this relationship with Him. It means that the creator of the universe is on our side, working alongside us, sharing in our daily lives. Out of this relationship with Him flow deeper relationships with those around us. Quite simply, our ability to impact the world for good is greatly enhanced if we hang out with God.

Perhaps you doubt that God is even real. That is no problem for God, for in this book you will find that God speaks to doubters and even to unbelievers. There are no barriers as far as God is concerned.

Could this be ESP, telepathy or something similar? The only proof that I have to offer you is, that I have been a follower of Christ for ten years and it was only after I became a follower of Christ at age 33 that God's Spirit was placed in me and this "ability" of mine surfaced. I had no ability to "know" things until that point. And as I continue to walk with Christ this ability to hear God grows stronger. I notice also that it is God Himself that initiates conversation in the vast majority of cases in this book. I also do not want to intimate that I am perfect. I am only human and we all make mistakes. Yet that does not dissuade me from pressing onward and trying to hear Him all the more clearly.

You can write this single episode off to coincidence perhaps, but I am going to present more emails to you in the hope that when the "coincidences" in this book begin to add up you will find that there is more to this than just "coincidence". At this point you do not even have to agree or disagree with me. All I am doing is asking you to look into this with an open mind, saying "yes this could possibly be God" because if you can do that, you will be on the right track. You can let the evidence stack up and then at the end ask yourself, "Is this really God after all? Is He really talking to us"?

Our God is a God of relationship and we will see in this book how God will often speak to us through other people. He does this by placing thoughts in their minds which they then speak out to us. It can greatly assist us in making decisions when we have the ability to discern when someone is speaking with Godly wisdom. When we find these people we need to listen very carefully to what they have to say, they will enrich our lives.

We so often forget that God is interested in even the small things of our lives. God was showing William that something he had done was pleasing to Him. Wouldn't you like to know that the things that you do are pleasing to God? Hearing from God like this, encouraged William that day. When you hear directly from God you will be encouraged in a way that no person on earth could ever encourage you. To have the creator of the universe pleased with you? Now that is exciting!

As you read this book you will begin to see that God is speaking all the time, and that He is speaking to many different people. In fact as you read the encounters described in this book you will realize that He is even speaking to you through them.

This book is filled with real life emails that I sent to people because I heard God speaking to me about them. The emails all contain a common thread of God's love for people and none of the emails is fictional; every one of them is real. They contain within them some of the normal daily struggles of life that we all go through. Some of the recipients are ordinary people, and some of them are church leaders. Perhaps you will be able to identify with some of the situations in which these people found themselves.

It is my hope that perhaps you will catch a glimpse of your life in some of these emails so that you will also be encouraged to draw near to God and learn His ways and so that you can hear Him speak to you too. I know that once you discover that the Creator of the Universe is interested in your life, your life will be transformed, and you will truly begin to live life to the fullest.

2. *God is in the big things.*

Moving on from the small things of God to the bigger things, things of monumental importance, things related to life and death. These are the big things in our lives, the things that if God really cares about us He surely must be interested in.

Chris is one of the senior pastors of a church with thousands of members, so you would expect Chris to know God and God to be interested in the things that Chris is involved with on a day to day basis. On the 13th of December Chris was very close to God, much closer than usual. And while I may bump into Chris at church once a month I need to emphasize that I don't know the day to day details of Chris' life. I had no idea what he was doing on that day. But God knew and God cared.

This is what I emailed to Chris at that time:

> From: markcraythorn@hotmail.com
>
> Sent: Wednesday, December 14, 2005 11:02 AM
>
> To: Chris@xxxxx.com
>
> Subject: God is with you
>
> Chris,
>
> The Lord gave me a dream about you last night so I know that he is with you right now in an even greater way than usual.
>
> Also the Lord wants you to know that he sees what you are doing. He sees how you come behind people to support

> them. He sees how you encourage others. He sees what
> you do to give others opportunity. This is the greatest form
> of self-sacrifice: thinking of others above yourself. You
> think that you are not being seen - but the Lord sees it all.
> He sees it all and He wants you to know it.
>
> God Bless
> ~Mark

While it is obvious that not all dreams are from God, God may nevertheless still choose to communicate to us through our dreams. For further support for the idea that dreams can come from God we need only look at the cases recorded in the Bible. Daniel and Joseph for example received many messages from God via their dreams. Daniel's dreams predicted the future and Joseph with his coat of many colors was hated all the more by his brothers for telling them his dream that they would bow down to him.

If we look at the Biblical dream messages we can see that they were often obscure and required special interpretation. The same is true today. Since dreams given by God are often in the language of symbols, pictures and stories; interpretation of God-given dreams requires wisdom from God.

God gives us dreams to engage us, so that we enquire what is going on. Questions arise in our minds and we begin to seek the answers. We may seek out other people in the hope that they have the answers but in the end the search ultimately ends in God. God wants to be found by us.

He wants so much to be found that we even see Biblical examples of people not following after Him who received dreams from Him. A case in point is that of King Nebuchadnezzar whose dreams troubled him. He searched and searched for the interpretation until he was directed to Daniel who was able to tell him both what he saw in his dream and the meaning thereof.

God and email.

In the Biblical account of Joseph and his Coat of Many Colors, God gave vivid dreams to Joseph in which He showed Joseph that his brothers would bow down to him, yet even though Joseph was able to interpret the dreams he failed to fully understand the timing of the event which would ultimately only come to pass many years in the future. So we see that God can choose to withhold from us the full meaning of the dreams that He has given us.

Even though Chris is very close to God, God still chose to withhold the full meaning of the message from Chris. So Chris replied with a thank you.

"Chris" <Chris@xxxxx.com>

01/03/2006 02:17 PM

Mark:

Thanks for the encouraging words. The example of Christ in Philippians 2 has always been a goal – to consider others as more important than myself. I know that God is aware of me all the time, but the reminder is good.

I hope you and your family had a great Christmas holiday.

See you soon. Blessings. Chris.

But I still pressed the point knowing that wasn't the real reason for God drawing close to Chris. I was looking for specifics and probed more deeply, sending this email:

From: markcraythorn@hotmail.com

Sent: Tuesday, January 03, 2006 2:31 PM

To: Chris

God and email.

Subject: RE: God is with you

Chris,

It is quite a few days ago but is there any reason that you can think of around Dec 13-14 that this might have been applicable? Anything special that you might have been doing? Involved in? Something happening personally? That is often the reason the Lord draws near to us.

Yes we did have a great Christmas holiday. My mother-in-law visited from South Africa and the whole family had a good time just being with her.

Blessings

~Mark

December 13-14? "What was going on then?" I began to wonder to myself. Why were those dates important? I had to wait until early January for this reply from Chris:

Mark:

On December 13th, my brother-in-law (Pete) and I went to see my cousin Ted with the hopes of sharing Christ with him. I hadn't seen Ted but a couple times in the past 20 years, but I knew he was dying of cancer at about age 45. He had also been a severe diabetic since childhood and had lost both legs to amputation. We were able to meet with him for about an hour or so. We talked a bit about heaven and that salvation was a free gift from God to those who believed in Jesus. We had the chance to pray for Ted as well and it seemed as though he participated in the prayer time. He indicated that he was trusting in Jesus for heaven although I'm not real sure how well formed his faith was – we'll need to leave that judgment to Jesus. But, we felt good about taking the time to go see him and hope our words and prayers helped him connect with Jesus. He died on 12/28 and I attended his funeral on 12/30.

I'm hoping that Ted trusted Jesus for forgiveness and eternal life. I'd hoped that he would live long enough to allow more dialogue, but Jesus is in control.

Nothing else comes to mind on those two days, but your word would certainly be an encouragement to Jim and me believing God told us to go see him. Thanks.

Blessings. Chris.

Now it all made sense! On December 13 Chris and Pete had gone to see Ted who was dying of cancer. There was a lot going on.

God had seen all of the pain, and out of death He was bringing hope and joy into the situation. He wanted to reassure Chris that He had heard his prayers.

God wanted to confirm to Chris that out of death comes life, eternal life. This was confirmation that even though Chris was "not real sure how well formed his (Ted's) faith was", that his cousin Ted is in heaven. What a confirmation! Confirmation from God Himself!

Another interesting fact is that Pete, Ted and Chris were all related – they were all "family". God has created the family and placed an extremely high value on it. Despite the fact that Chris hadn't seen Ted more than "a couple of times in 20 years", God was interested in Chris' relationship with his cousin Ted. Out of the coming together of family members that had not seen each other much in 20 years, God brought restoration and life. God wants us to take note and to see the value He places on relationships between family members.

If you have not spoken to family members in a long time, God wants you to know that He is very interested in restoring those relationships too. God wanted to bless Chris for reaching across that 20 year gap. God will bless you too if you reach across the gap to someone in your family with whom you have a strained or limited relationship.

Just as God is concerned about our relationship with our family members, God is concerned about our relationship with Him too. No matter how near to Him we are, or how far away from Him we may have drifted, God wants to draw us further in towards Him. He is always calling us into closer and closer relationship with Himself.

God cared for Ted to the end. The parallel message for those of you who are sick, or in pain, is that God wants you to know that He sees your pain, and is concerned about you too.

We have all at some time or other prayed and wondered where God is and why he doesn't answer our prayers. God wants you to know that He is hearing all of your prayers. In fact even if you forget to pray, or possibly don't feel like praying, He still hears the unspoken groaning and yearning of your heart. God is always listening to your sincere prayers from the heart because He is always interested in you. He will answer your prayers in His way, in His time, in the manner that is best suited for you.

Finally, God wants you to know that if you pray, He will hear your prayers. If you pray He will be there; it is prayer that opens a pathway between us and God.

The key to God hearing these prayers and responding in such a powerful way was that those praying expressed faith in Jesus. If you want God to hear your prayers and respond in such a powerful way in your life then you need to get to know this Jesus too. He is the key that unlocks the door.

3.   *God is the author of life.*

Bill and his wife Shannon, young newlyweds, live in Houston where Bill has recently started a new, vibrant church. They are regularly expecting God to do big things on their behalf. God began talking to me about children in Bill's life. Despite not having emailed or spoken to Bill in over a year, I was able to recognize the whisper from God and decided to find out more about these children in Bill's life. I dug his email address out and sent this brief email:

> From: Mark Craythorn (markcraythorn@hotmail.com)
> Sent: Tue 2/06/07 8:53 PM
> To: bill@xxxxxx.com
> Subject: Children
>
> Hi Bill,
>
> The Lord is very close to you now. He is speaking to me about you and children. I think He wants me to ask you about this and what it means.
>
> Let me know what is going on.
> God Bless
> ~Mark

And Bill responded with the exciting news that he and Shannon were expecting their first baby. Interestingly this email came on the day they found out that their baby would be a girl:

> Re: Children
> From: Pastor Bill (bill@xxxxxx.com)
> Sent:Tue 2/06/07 10:42 PM
> To: Mark Craythorn (markcraythorn@hotmail.com)
>
> Mark,

God and email.

Great to hear from you! God's timing is always amazing - thanks for being obedient to the leading and emailing me to ask about it. Shannon and I are actually expecting our first child - she is due June 20. Today was our midpoint ultrasound/anatomy scan, and we just found out this morning that we are having a baby girl! I couldn't be more thrilled - we are so happy to be welcoming a child into our family. That is where we are at right now - if God is telling you anything about the situation I would love to hear about it.

I'd also love for you to explain more about what you said about the Lord being very close to me now. I just completed a time of fasting last week, and we are believing God for some HUGE things in our church right now - I've sensed that we are on the verge of something. I'd love for you to tell me what you've been hearing in that area as well.

How have you been? How is your family doing? Are you back in the States? I would love to catch up and hear what's been going on in your life and ministry lately. Thanks for emailing - looking forward to talking more.

Bill
Lead Pastor
xxxxxx.com

God wants us to know that He is the author of life. He is the one who knew that Shannon was pregnant and He wanted both Bill and her to know that He was rejoicing in this pregnancy together with them.

If God is so interested in babies then it stands to reason that the life that He has put in us is to be nurtured and treasured. It should cause us to look at one another anew in reverence and awe and to treat each other with the dignity and respect that this knowledge brings.

God's speaking to Bill coincided with Bill just ending a fast where he had petitioned God for "HUGE things" in his church. We learn from this episode that we can fast from food and pray in order to draw closer to God. God had seen Bill's desire to get closer to Him and had responded by touching Bill in a place of real intimacy. A place that was much more personal than even Bill could have expected.

I am sure that huge things will happen in Bill's church; God responds to us when we seek Him with Bill's intensity. The message that comes through loud and clear is that God is much more interested in us than He is in the church. It is primarily the people that make up the church that God is interested in.

Since God is so intensely interested in people, it also means that God is intensely interested in you. Just as He authored Bill and his wife's baby, He also authored your life. God was watching over your life from the start and since then has watched over every second of it. Surely He is watching over it now.

Perhaps you think that these situations where God reaches out to us are all very good for other people, especially those who are pastors, but that they don't apply to you. Perhaps you think that you are different to the ministers, pastors and other great people of faith and you are asking yourself if God could ever really be that interested in your life.

If you think that your life is pretty ordinary, then I think the story of Sam and Kate should interest you. They are two "ordinary" people from South Carolina whose only daughter Katelyn recently got married. What does stand out about Sam and Kate, however, is that they have taken time over the years to get to know God better. They have in the process formed a relationship with the living God. It is a relationship borne of time, a relationship that any of us can begin at any time.

God and email.

It had been many, many months since I last heard from them. Hearing again that whisper from God, I sensed God telling me that His presence had moved into their lives in a greater way than usual and that their daughter Katelyn was involved. There was only one way to find out what was happening in their lives:

From: markcraythorn@hotmail.com
To: kate@xxxxx.com; sam@xxxxx.com
Sent: Tue, 10 Apr 2007 10:11 AM
Subject: God with you

Just wanted to say that I really felt that the Lord's presence was with you in a much stronger way than usual this weekend. So anyway just wanted to write and let you know that.

How is Katelyn doing? You spend time with her recently?

On our end things are quiet. Our family is going to S. Africa in 2 months time and will be spending a month there so we are looking forward to that.

Blessings in Christ
~Mark

Kate responded by announcing that they were expecting their first grandchild. The due date had been Sunday the 8th, in line with the "weekend" that I had mentioned in my email. I would expect that emotions had run high in their family that weekend as they anticipated the new arrival. Now a few days late Katelyn's baby was going to be induced the very next day:

To: markcraythorn@hotmail.com
Subject: Re: God with you
Date: Wed, 11 Apr 2007 16:39:39 -0400
From: kate@xxxxx.com

> Mark, thanks for your email. Your sense of the Lord's presence is accurate. We are in Jackson, MS, with Katelyn and Ted, who are expecting their first baby, a boy. It (he) was due the 8th, but not here yet. Katelyn is to be inducecd tomorrow morning (April 12), and we will just wait some more till Master Marvin apprears. Thank you again for your interest, concern, and PRAYERS. Will keep you posted.
>
> Kitty

God was trying to show everyone that He was fully aware of the impending birth, but more importantly, God was reaching out to bring reassurance that all would be well. Kate was easily able to recognize God in that exciting time in their lives. God is the giver of life and He had chosen to celebrate that life along with their family. He obviously delighted in showing that He knew about the birth and bringing reassurance that everything was going to work out just fine.

> From: markcraythorn@hotmail.com
> To: kate@xxxxx.com
> Sent: Wed, 11 Apr 2007 9:45 PM
> Subject: RE: God with you
>
> That is wonderful. You must be so excited. Our daughter Melissa was born in Jackson too. We lived there for about 18 months but that seems like a lifetime ago.
>
> My prayers go out to her tomorrow & to you too.
>
> God Bless
> ~Mark

The outcome of all of this is that Sam & Kate are now proud grandparents of a beautiful baby boy. Once again God was authoring life and then celebrating that life with those He loves.

But there is another message tucked away in all of this. Children, parents and grandparents are all involved in this story; God wants to emphasize to us His love for the entire family. God loves families! He creates families and He celebrates the life in them. He laughs with us when we laugh and He cries with us when we cry. The nature and character of God is such that He wants the best for your family too.

So whether you are a pastor, a minister or just an "ordinary" person, God wants to celebrate your life as well. Will you draw near to God, the author of life, and allow Him to do that?

4. *God is always interested in us*

You may be looking at the story of Sam & Kate in the previous chapter and saying to yourself that "this is still not my situation, my situation is different". Perhaps you don't even believe in God like Sam & Kate do. You have not had time to get to know God like they have, so you are asking yourself, "why on earth would God be interested in me? ".

Michael is my cousin and Michael's concept of God is far, far removed from my concept of God. That doesn't stop God. God is not intimidated by that. God is much too large to be intimidated by anything as small as our attitudes and beliefs towards Him.

In this email God had been showing me that He was suddenly more interested than usual in my cousin. God was trying to show that He cared about a specific situation in Michael's life. I wanted to find out what the reason for God's interest was and there was only one way to find out: I needed to ask my cousin Michael.

From: mark.craythorn@hotmail.com
To: Michael@xxxxxx.com
Subject: Hi
Date: Fri, 16 Jun 2006 11:02:06 -0400

Seems like God is looking with interest at you again - you see we might think that we are alone but we never really are. He cares too much for us to leave us alone.

~Mark

It turned out that his sister Vicky living in South Africa had had her house invaded by three men carrying guns – *tsotsis* in South African parlance. She had not been there but her maid and three children had been pretty badly shaken by the incident.

> From: "Michael" <Michael@xxxxxx.com>
> 06/25/2006 06:33 PM
> To: markcraythorn@hotmail.com
> Subject: RE: Hi
>
> The timing certainly had me thinking for a few days - uncanny .....
> But - demons and my chaotic life aside - Vicky had a home invasion - they were at work and the maid got hit by 3 gun toting tsotsi's whilst watching the kids - pretty serious – everyone's shaken up.
> ....

Michael did say that the timing of this email was "uncanny" but then he also went on to say:

> But back to the gospels of mark - i still don't quite know what to make of your faith or of the question of religion - it returns every so oft and it's not so much the issue of a deity - i do actually believe that there is an all encompassing being - i just have an issue as to what to do about it and certainly have no desire to mix with the confused humans that try to worship
>
> ....
>
> confusing

He admitted that he didn't know what to make of my faith or even of religion. He summed it all up in one word "confusing". But God hadn't been intimidated by his uncertainty and confusion. God was still trying to show that He cared. The big question was whether Michael would decide whether the coincidence of my email's arrival was evidence of God at work or not.

God and email.

God never, ever gives up. Eleven months later God was still waiting for another opportunity to show Michael that He cared for him & his family. But that's the next story.

5. *God is not intimidated by unbelief*

God is not intimidated by our level of unbelief in him, and has a remarkable level of patience with us. We may be going through our lives blissfully unaware of God's interest in us but He is always waiting for us to turn towards Him.

God remained close to Michael my cousin for the next eleven months after the previous story until this, the next chapter of God's interest in Michael, unfolded. Michael has a brother Steve. It stands to reason then that if God is interested in Michael then He would be interested in Michael's family relationships and thus would be interested in Steve too. What unfolded was another case of God showing how He patiently waits for us in our wanderings and even our unbelief until He can again draw us to Himself. This time He also underlined again just how interested he is in families.

God showed me that my cousin Steve, who I have had no contact with in many years and have no phone number or email address for, was going through a difficult time. So out of concern I emailed Michael to try and find out what was going on:

From: Mark Craythorn markcraythorn@hotmail.com
To: "Michael@xxxxxx.com" Michael@xxxxxx.com
Subject: Steve
Date: Mon, 21 May 2007 09:05:36 -0400

Hi Michael,
Have you heard from Steve lately?
~Mark

Two subsequent emails from Michael revealed that his brother Steve was in a bad way:

God and email.

From: Michael@xxxxxx.com
To: markcraythorn@hotmail.com
Subject: RE: Steve
Date: Mon, 21 May 2007 14:14:38 +0000

i can only assume u meant my brother? if so - yeah -
partied with him on his 40th 2
weeks back spoke to him on Friday.

he's not a happy chappie methinx
..... lotsa drama and <*&!#@>.

RE: Steve
From: Michael (Michael@xxxxxx.com)
Sent:Tue 5/22/07 4:38 AM
To: markcraythorn@hotmail.com

......

 I'm not sure what steve's issues are - but he appears more
lost than me - i've always had the solace of books and
work to sink into - he doesn't - and also doesn't have the
same capability to be on his own.
I can guess at a few things that's probably spiralling him
down - but my history with him makes it difficult as he
was around when i spun out .....
He has alot of issues to deal with ad has no real hobbies or
friends - i couldn't be bothered with ppl either, but i've just
got a new surf board and a few things I still want to try out,
so kinda have some light at the end - if i so desire - i fear
that he has none.

But - be that as it may - I hope to try and get closer once i
return to CT from the US ...

Your 'contacts' are good ...... do they do Lotto numbers?
ciao
MikeD

God and email.

Michael had admitted that his life had "spun out" in the past. He could identify with his brother's pain as his brother went through essentially the same situation that Michael had been through some years back. God was putting someone in Steve's life that could identify with that pain, someone who had a little "light at the end" of the tunnel.

Michael's final comment, "Your 'contacts' are good ...... do they do Lotto numbers?" made me chuckle. It showed his recognition that something greater was at work, something that defied explanation. At this point I still don't know how the story will turn out but what I do know beyond a shadow of a doubt is that God is not finished with this story just yet.

6.   *God answers prayers*

At some time or other we have all wondered why God doesn't seem to hear our prayers. There are times when we think that He doesn't exist or doesn't care about us. And we wonder why God apparently doesn't get involved in the things going on in this world. There is so much injustice, hurt and pain that needs to be set right. As puzzling as these questions are to us, there are also the times when He does step in and immediately answer our prayers, causing us to stand awed and amazed with renewed hope and trust in His goodness. It is times like this that cause us to begin to pray with renewed fervor in the conviction that God does in fact hear our prayers.

My sister in law Daphne, living in South Africa, was having a difficult time trying to sell her house. She had been trying unsuccessfully for many, many weeks to sell it and now this important financial decision was spilling over into her daily life and creating a lot of tension. The love of money may be the root of all evil, but money is always such an important issue in our lives, that it should come as no surprise that God is very, very interested in our attitudes towards money. I have found it helpful as far as money is concerned, to always keep my focus on God rather than money as this often helps the money problems to recede into the background and resolve themselves. Daphne had got to a point where she felt that her back was up against a wall financially. It is at times like this, where we have exhausted our own efforts, that in our desperation, it helps to turn to God.

From my prayers, I already had a sense that God was up to something as far as Daphne's house was concerned, nevertheless, I prayed earnestly that day for God to help her sell her house and then taking another step suggested that she do the same:

God and email.

From: markcraythorn@hotmail.com
<mark.craythorn@hotmail.com>
Sent: 6/1/06 4:04:51 PM
To: "Daphne@xxxxxx.com"<Daphne@xxxxxx.com>
Subject: house

Hi Daph,

Lisa tells me you are having trouble selling. That started me thinking and my thoughts went something like this.....

God is obviously in this process. I have seen that already and I think you have at least considered that too after my phone call. So if God is in something that is a good thing - He wants things to work out for our good.

So why hasn't it sold yet? Well have you asked God to get you a buyer? He can move mountains if we ask so all we have to do is ask. I asked for it last night. I think you should too.

....

The very next day she emailed me back excitedly. The house was as good as sold. God answered that prayer within 24 hours.

From: "Daphne@xxxxxx.com" <Daphne@xxxxxx.com>
06/01/2006 02:51 PM
To:mark.craythorn@hotmail.com
Subject: RE: house

Hi Mark,
I GOT AN OFFER ON MY HOUSE!!!!!! Thanks for the email that you sent, it made me feel so much better. One of the people that viewed my place last night phoned this morning to say that she wanted to put an offer in, I tried not to get too excited in case it didn't happen. Anyway, the agent phoned tonight because she was busy doing the offer with the buyer so it has finally happened!!

I'm meeting with the agent tomorrow to sign it off if I'm happy with it. I'll let you know what happens tomorrow.
Thanks for all the prayers and kind words....
Love
Daph

I could almost feel the excitement expressed in that email. God helped her sell her house. I find it delightful that Daphne doesn't attend church but God still took the time to answer those prayers. It shows us that God is intensely interested in all of us and especially so when we go through difficult times.

It is also interesting that the prayers and email made her "feel so much better". When God steps in and answers prayers it often energizes us. If for no other reason that this we should pray with sincerity and conviction looking for God to answer our prayers so that we can be revitalized again and again with more and more answered prayers.

7.   *God in the special days of life*

God has a special place reserved for those that do work for Him and try to make His name known. Andrew is a missionary from the USA working in Ghana, Africa. He is accompanied by his Brazilian wife Juliana (Ju) who is a doctor and works at a medical clinic. They have two young children who are a blessing to them. Andrew and I originally met while attending a Discipleship Training School with Youth With A Mission (YWAM) in Scotland, and have kept in touch occasionally over the years.

One night God gave me a dream about Andrew. In it He showed me that there was a lot going on in Andrew's life but one thing in particular really stood out:

From: Mark Craythorn
[mailto:markcraythorn@hotmail.com]
Sent: Saturday, March 31, 2007 7:38 PM
To: Andrew@xxxxx.com
Subject: what's up?

Hey Andrew,

What's going on on your side of the ocean? The Lord gave me a dream about you last night. So I think He wants to encourage you. What ministry activities are you involved with right now?

There is something in this regarding other people who will be going to the same place / doing the same thing with you.

......

Blessings in Christ my brother.

~Mark

From: Andrew@xxxxx.com
To: markcraythorn@hotmail.com
Subject: RE: what's up?
Date: Sun, 1 Apr 2007 09:46:10 +0000

Mark,

SO good to hear from you!

We are working and loving the Lord here in Ghana.

…. We have TODAY, a group of Americans arriving today for 24-36 hours. They are an advance team to see if they want to bring a big team next year and do a work project.
……
Saturday I turned 34 years old, and I'm SO blessed.

We've not had electricity for about 2 weeks now – and the Lord is giving us the strength. Lord willing we will have a generator installed this month.

I must go, will write more when I hear back.
How can we pray for you all?

Blessings to you,
Andrew

Andrew's response was that there was a group of Americans arriving the day that He received the email. The dream obviously related to that. But another detail that was so amazing to me was that Andrew had also had a birthday on the day that I dreamed about him. One thing that I have learned about God is that He is so very interested in the intricate details of our lives and something as significant as a birthday is something as special to us as it is to God himself.

From: Mark Craythorn
[mailto:markcraythorn@hotmail.com]
Sent: Tuesday, April 03, 2007 12:52 AM
To: Andrew@xxxxx.com
Subject: RE: what's up?

Hi Andrew,

This is what I think:

     Since I had the dream on the night of your birthday - the Lord wants to show you that He even knows about your birthday. So happy birthday!!!!!!!!!!
     I think that the group of Americans arriving at the same time as the dream is significant - you should pay close attention to that.

....

Be blessed my brother
In Christ
~Mark

Another small detail that God had not overlooked was that when I had had a birthday six months previously Andrew had sent me an email congratulating me. It had caught me by surprise since we were not in the habit of exchanging birthday greetings and I didn't really ever recall having received one from him before. God was now returning the favor and surprising Andrew by remembering him on his birthday. The ways of God continue to astound me.

RE: what's up?
From: Andrew (andrew@xxxxx.com)
Sent:Sun 4/08/07 8:43 AM
Reply-to:Andrew@xxxxx.com

To: 'Mark Craythorn' (markcraythorn@hotmail.com)

God and email.

Wow!

Hi there! We can receive this for us. Ju, my dreamer, read your notes and definitely said it was from the Lord.

We are in Kumasi for the weekend and we have been able to have some time with electricity and… internet. We got back to the village today.
....

Be blessed and give your family our love please please please.

Love to you,
Andrew and Ju

Andrew and his wife Ju's response summed up in "Wow!" shows that they recognized this as something that had come from God and received it as such. They are open and willing to receive from God so it does not surprise me that God chose to draw near to them.

The reason that God speaks to us today is to continually draw us to Him and this was no exception. I am sure they felt a little closer to God after this. Isn't it nice to know that your birthday is known and remembered by God?

8. *God in the normal days of life*

I first met Ini in a hotel in Houston. He worked nights behind the front desk, and since that was generally a quiet time in the hotel, was using that time to study towards becoming a medical doctor. He eventually completed those studies graduating way near the top of the class. He accepted a medical residency in Chicago and I had not heard from him for some time; but God never forgets us, he is always with us, sometimes more so during the "normal" days of our lives.

Often as we go through life we go through more difficult, stress filled times and, whether we know it or not, God draws nearer to us during times like this. I sensed something like this happening in Ini's life but I had no idea why this might be so. I ended up sending him a simple short message along the lines of "God is with you".

Ini's response was that he was going to write his final medical board exam soon and was under a lot of pressure juggling that with the long hours involved in his medical residency program. He was also looking for a hospital that would accept him as a doctor upon completion of his board exam. There was definitely a lot on his mind. All I could say was that I would pray for him.

He need not have worried, God was with him and he ended up doing extremely well in the exam, graduating with excellent grades. His hard work over the years was rewarded and he was subsequently also offered a position as a medical doctor at an excellent hospital.

Ini expressed his gratitude for my simple email in this message below:

> From: Ini@xxxxxx.com
> To: markcraythorn@hotmail.com

Subject: Hello!
Date: Tue, 22 Aug 2006 04:47:10 +0000

Hello Mark and Lisa,
How are you guys doing? Hope very good. I hope the ministry is doing well. Thanks for praying for me two months ago. At that time I was facing job interviews and a board exam and was under quite a bit of pressure. The word that God is with me coming from you really came at a good time. I ended up getting the job and doing well in the board exam. Thanks again.
....
Take care of yourselves and hope you can reply soon.
Ini

Ini gave thanks for the word from God that came providing reassurance at a crucial time in his life. By myself I would not have known what was up in Ini's life but God did, God cared and God wanted Ini to know that He had been with him through the entire stress filled time. Looking back one can only give thanks to God that He cared for Ini in the "normal" days of his life.

9. God is with us at work

By now you have probably noticed that there is something that defies coincidence behind all of these emails. Even if you are unsure whether or not God exists you would have to acknowledge that there is something beyond explanation going on. The case for the existence of God is getting very good indeed as is the case for His willingness and ability to speak into our lives.

Peter was the COO/CEO of a successful computer consulting company based in Atlanta. He ran the company in that capacity for sixteen years and was skilled at what he did. Despite his success, extremely prominent people in the company became involved in illegal financial dealings and had to appear in federal court on charges of conspiracy, wire fraud and even theft of federal funds. Peter suddenly found himself facing the possibility of many years in prison.

Before the case went to trial Peter was offered a plea bargain in which he was given the option to plead guilty to some of the charges. Doing so would reduce the severity of the eventual sentence and Peter was old enough at that point that if he accepted the plea bargain he would not have gone to prison. Still Peter would have ended up with a criminal record and that was unacceptable to him.

Peter knew in his heart that he was innocent; he had not maliciously set out to defraud anyone, and therefore rejected the plea bargain on principle.

Now after rejecting the plea bargain, the odds were heavily stacked against Peter and he knew it. He was in all probability going on trial in a federal court and faced the possibility that he would go to prison for many years. Things were not looking good.

The first I knew about all of this was when God told me that Peter was in "financial difficulties"; an understatement to say the least. I knew Peter's character from having worked with him and knew that he would not knowingly have become involved in illegal activities. Peter would probably have said that he was skeptical about God at this point but that wasn't important. What was important was that God knew Peter's predicament.

I contacted Peter who I had not emailed in months, possibly even in a year, to ask him what the details of the situation were. He explained it all to me over the phone. I tried to show him that God was involved: how else would I have known to call him?

Over the next few months God walked with Peter whether he knew it or not. Over time I had a couple more phone conversations with Peter and tried to reassure Him that God had shown me that he was innocent. On other days I just sent an encouraging email:

From: markcraythorn@hotmail.com
Sent: Monday, April 24, 2006 3:17 PM
To: Peter@xxxxxx.com
Subject: lawsuit

Hi Peter,

… you are on my mind a lot today. How is it going with the pending lawsuit?

Regards
~Mark

Through the continued prayers, God was there through the entire process, even when the jury was being selected. Peter expressed thanks for my "positive thoughts", i.e. prayers, on his behalf:

From: "Peter" <Peter@xxxxxx.com>

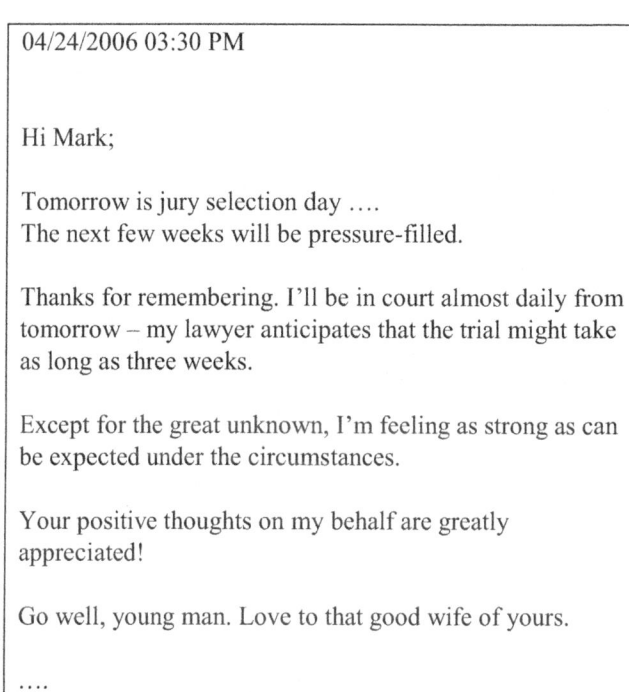

04/24/2006 03:30 PM

Hi Mark;

Tomorrow is jury selection day ….
The next few weeks will be pressure-filled.

Thanks for remembering. I'll be in court almost daily from
tomorrow – my lawyer anticipates that the trial might take
as long as three weeks.

Except for the great unknown, I'm feeling as strong as can
be expected under the circumstances.

Your positive thoughts on my behalf are greatly
appreciated!

Go well, young man. Love to that good wife of yours.

….

Peter.

It is one thing to know that God sees that you are innocent
but it is quite another thing to prove that in a jury trial. I wasn't
sure what the jury decision would be. Regardless of whether
or not God knew that Peter was innocent I had no idea how
this was going to play out. I continued to pray for Peter.

Days before the trial verdict, I prayed for favor from the jury. I
prayed that they would see Peter's innocence. Others
continued to pray too. Interestingly the jurors also admitted
that they had had prayer during deliberations to come up with
the right verdict. They were not easy days for Peter. To me
he described the day when he rose to hear the verdict as "the
scariest day of my life".

Six of those involved were found guilty and sentenced to many years in prison, yet when he arose in court to hear the verdict read to him, Peter was pronounced "not guilty". He breathed a sigh of relief.

In a series of emails to me, after the verdict was handed down, Peter acknowledged in his own way that there was more than coincidence at work here:

From: "Peter" <Peter@xxxxxx.com>
06/01/2006 04:54 PM
To: <mark.craythorn@hotmail.com>
Subject: The Power of Prayer

Hey, you're good at this! Maybe a consulting practice
....

Spoken like a true consultant Peter! In the months to come, Peter visited his daughter in New Jersey and went to church with her for the first time. Peter admitted that there had been nothing remarkable about his visit to church but that he had "enjoyed it". For someone who had made a point of not visiting church in the past, something deeper and more profound had indeed happened. God was reconciling Peter to Himself and continues to do so.

10. *God helps financially*

We all want more money. We dream of winning the lottery and try to imagine what we would do with our winnings. The reality is that you are probably buffeted daily by demands on your finances and it seems that no matter how much money you have you always need more. The Bible often talks about money, so it should come as no surprise to you that God is very interested in your finances.

A good starting point when dealing with finances is to take a step back and remember that everything that you receive in the way of finances is actually a gift from God.

God gives you gifts to bless you. He doesn't want you to hoard up your gifts; He would like you to use them. Be careful how you use them though, the manner in which you use your money is a good reflection of the condition of your heart as it reveals either your selfish nature or your generous nature.

God warns us to use our money wisely. There is a parable in the Bible of three servants. One was given 1 talent (a unit of coinage in those days), another 2 talents and another 5 talents. The servants who were given 2 and 5 talents both managed to increase them and Jesus called them good and faithful servants. They were put in charge of many things and shared in their master's happiness. But the one with 1 talent was afraid and went out and hid his money in the ground. Jesus called him a worthless servant. God expects us to do more than the worthless servant and to take good care of that with which he has entrusted us.

Gary was concerned about the money that he had been entrusted with. He had been invited to attend a Christian Micro Enterprise Development conference in Peru. He wanted to take his wife with him but was concerned that this might be extravagant. He wanted to be prudent in the use of his money. But probably the biggest hurdle that Gary faced was that the money that he had was not enough for two trans-continental plane tickets and living expenses in a foreign country.

Gary wanted to be sure to use God's resources wisely:

To: markcraythorn@hotmail.com
Subject: Requests for help
From: Gary@xxxxx.com
Date: Thu, 12 Apr 2007 18:34:47 -0400

Hi!

We urgently need whatever input you might have for us. Here's the situation: within the next few days we need to make a decision about attending the Micro-enterprise Development conference in Peru. If both of us go, the cost will be double and we only could cover a small portion from our personal resources. The big question: how many folks would be willing to help financially so that both of us can go? We're asking because we believe God wants us to have your input before we decide. If you would consider financial support for this, please let us know right away (the total cost is about $4,000). If not, that is fine...we honestly just want God's direction on this, which is why we're "putting out the fleece."

......

Thanks for listening--we deeply appreciate each dollar of support, each prayer, each encouraging email or note!

Under His mercy,

Gary and Peggy
(ps as always, if you have any questions or prefer to not receive email appeals from us, please tell us!)

God and email.

Gary
XXXXXXX Ministries
XXXXXXX University

But there was something that Gary had overlooked. He had been invited to attend, he had therefore been called by God, and where God calls you to do something He will provide a way for you to do it.

On Apr 12, 2007, at 9:59 PM, Mark Craythorn wrote:

Gary,

If you believe with all your heart that God has called you both to go, then go even if the financial resources are not there. God has a way of rewarding faith of that nature by providing blessings from unexpected sources and in ways that you would not have anticipated. For example you may be approached only after you get back by someone with a job that provides for the money that you need. But note that the blessing most often only comes AFTER you step out in faith. But here is the key : you must firmly believe that what you are doing will enhance the kingdom.

And in the end whatever you decide - if you do it believing that God has called you to do it: He will bless that!!!

In Christ
~Mark

Gary still wasn't fully convinced. Understandably He was still cautious:

From: Gary@xxxxx.com
Subject: Re: Requests for help
Date: Tue, 17 Apr 2007 17:48:26 -0400
To: markcraythorn@hotmail.com

Mark,

Thanks for the helpful thoughts. You remind me of my Plymouth Brethren friends, who formed the heart of our financial support when we were in Moldova 1996-98 (and still do). When it came time to buy tickets (for 5 people-- our 3 youngest went with us), we didn't come close to Intervarsity's policy for amount of committed support, but praise God, IV had a VP who understood and respected PB ideas (you go, we'll support you, but don't ask us to sign a pledge card) and we were allowed to buy the tickets. After the first year in Moldova, contributions matched expenses within one dollar (total of $40K plus).

But God doesn't always work in the same way. Confirmation that we're truly pursuing God's agenda, not ours, has sometimes come in the form of financial support. For me, there are often tensions in the ways of God, one of them being discerning what is of faith and what isn't.

Peggy feels strongly about not going into debt so she is looking for assurance that she should go with me (I'm more involved with MED than her).

....

Under His mercy,

Gary

So Gary waited another month. He still wasn't sure what to do but He still felt that both he and his wife should go to the conference so they purchased the two plane tickets.

From: Gary@xxxxx.com
Subject: Peru trip update
Date: Tue, 15 May 2007 18:34:39 -0400
To: markcraythorn@hotmail.com

Dear family and friends,

God and email.

....

We really appreciate each one who took the time to email back, or call,
or talk with us. In a special way we value those who said they were
unable to help financially but still encouraged us to go.

About a week ago we felt that we had the Lord's mind to go and
yesterday I purchased tickets, so now we are committed! God willing, we
will leave July 26 for Cuzco, Peru and return home on August 9.

This will be a working trip as both of us plan to share in helping with
the training and other needs of the conference participants.

......

Under His mercy,

Gary

God can give us wisdom and help us to make right decisions if we turn our lives over to Him. We need to walk humbly in submission to God. If we can do that then circumstances will fall into place around us.

Gary had taken the important step of stepping out in faith believing that God had called him. He clearly says that he felt that he had "the Lord's mind" to go. We need to remember that when we step out in faith believing that God has called us to do something then that faith ignites something in the heart of God and He will move mountains to assist us.

Gary was going to be assisting others at the conference too. He was going with the heart of a servant. This was going to be work as well as pleasure. Gary was going for all the right reasons and God knew that.

Our next two email exchanges were brief.

> On May 15, 2007, at 9:20 PM, Mark Craythorn wrote:
>
> Exciting times!!!! Good decision. Now go have fun there too. :-)
>
> God Bless
> ~Mark

> From: Gary (Gary@xxxxx.com)
> Sent: Wed 5/16/07 3:59 PM
> To: Mark Craythorn (markcraythorn@hotmail.com)
> Subject: Peru trip update
>
> thanks, Mark. your input was valuable in this process!
>
> Gary

Neither of us was fully prepared for what happened next:

> From: Gary (Gary@xxxxx.com)
> Sent: Fri 5/25/07 4:21 PM
> To: Mark Craythorn (markcraythorn@hotmail.com)
> Subject: Peru
>
> Hi Mark,
>
> Yesterday I had a call from Belfast, N Ireland, from Andrew, one
> of the IFES guys who worked with us in Moldova. We spent some time with him and his parents during my 2004 sabbatical.
>
> He told me his parents have just received an inheritance and are
> planning to contribute 1000 pounds sterling (almost $2K at

> current
> exchange rates) to us for our travel to Peru.
>
> I'm sure you aren't surprised...
>
> Gary

Yes that summed it up – God had made a way, I was not surprised. God likes to provide unexpected solutions to our dilemmas and He likes to do it in a way that circumvents our natural ability to control or manipulate a situation. It ultimately shows us that He is in control.

But even this was not the end of the story, there was more to come:

> Peru
> From: Gary (Gary@xxxxx.com)
> Sent:Sat 6/02/07 3:30 PM
> To: Mark Craythorn (markcraythorn@hotmail.com)
>
> Hi Mark,
>
> The check from our friends in N Ireland came today, with a note that included a ref to Phil 4:19. The check was twice what we expected, over $3900. We are almost in shock...Peggy had tears in her eyes. If either of us had any lingering doubts that God wants both of us to go, they are no more.
>
> I thought that I didn't really need your emails to tell me to step out in faith, I knew if it was his will that God would provide. But this provision reveals how little confidence I really have in God. Not just the amount, but the who and where it came from.
>
> Under His mercy,
>
> Gary

God provided all the finances that Gary had been concerned about. It was to all extents and purposes the exact amount that Gary needed for both he & his wife to attend the conference. It was just like God to exceed our expectations over and above what we ever could have imagined.

You may struggle with your finances or with decisions on how to use your money wisely, but when God calls you to do something with your money then that call overrides all else. It is interesting to note that as in Gary's case, God's call is often not that dramatic and we are left puzzling over whether the intended course of action is in fact a call from God.

God waited and waited for over a month to see what Gary would do and only blessed Gary's faith after Gary stepped out in obedience to the call. Only after he had done all that he could by scraping together what money he could and purchasing two tickets, did God confirm in a magnificent way that it was his voice that Gary had responded to. It took Gary's purchase of the plane tickets to prove that he was setting himself up to go and this in turn set in motion the events that would ensure that he received the necessary money for the trip.

In my experience God always delights in sending blessings from unexpected sources. He seldom does the exact same thing twice. This shows us how much He loves variety but it also forces us away from formulas and patterns of approaching Him. It causes us to approach Him with nothing other than our childlike faith and trust in His goodness.

God delights in showing us that He has unlimited resources at His disposal. If the ways in which He is able to answer our prayers is unlimited, that alone should encourage us to pray bigger prayers.

And as He so often does, God used others in Gary's life. Our God is a God of relationship: He likes us to work together with others to achieve great things together. That way we can celebrate our successes together too.

God and email.

I wasn't surprised that God had so obviously stepped in. It was the manner in which He had done so and the sheer extravagance of it that caught me off guard. Our God is an extravagant God.

11. *God draws near to the sick*

Sometimes God places within my heart a deep desire to pray for someone and I just know deep inside myself that they are not well. In many cases these people that I pray for are sick, sometimes with something as minor as a cold, sometimes it is much worse. I had worked with Larry for over a year but had moved on from that job and had not seen him for almost five months. The latest burden that I felt for Larry just wouldn't go away despite ongoing prayer. So I wanted to find out what was going on with him:

> From: Mark Craythorn (markcraythorn@hotmail.com)
> Sent: Sat 5/05/07 4:42 PM
> To: Larry@xxxxx.com
>
> Hey Larry,
> Been thinking about you a lot these past 2 weeks.
> …..
> Cheers
> ~Mark

Larry's reply two weeks later confirmed that he had been suffering from a kidney stone which had ended up putting him in hospital. All of this coincided with the time that I felt a burden to pray for him.

> From: Larry@xxxxx.com
> Sent: Wed 5/16/07 8:34 AM
> To: Mark Craythorn (markcraythorn@hotmail.com)
> Subject: Re: Hi Larry
>
> Hello Mark,
> Sorry for the poor reply. I've been in a bad way the last few weeks. I was in the hospital 2 weeks back having a Kidney stone removed

God and email.

> ......
>
> Larry

I have seen God heal through prayer before, yet this time it was not to be, Larry was not physically healed and had to undergo surgery. Healing was to be slower and more painful. All I can say is that God was with Larry through this experience and wanted Larry to know it.

We need to trust in the goodness of God and look deeper into the situation. God knows our concerns and has the power to do something to alleviate our pain and suffering.

An interesting thing about Larry's situation is that Larry has struggled to walk for years after a military injury left him minus one of his spinal vertebrae. He was often using a cane to get about the last time that I saw him.

The doctors involved in the kidney stone operation also presented Larry with some new options for additional surgery to his spine that could improve his ability to walk. In the end though the choice was made for Larry and he was forced to undergo additional surgery:

> To: markcraythorn@hotmail.com
> Subject: RE: Hi Larry
> From: Larry@xxxxx.com
> Date: Mon, 25 Jun 2007 11:29:08 -0400
>
> The choice was made for me. I lost most feeling from the waist down and had to have emergency surgery a few weeks back. Once they opened me up to remove a small portion of disk they found that the Lamina was crushed. The 40 min surgery ended up taking over 2hrs and they had to remove the lamina (the bony covering protects the spinal cord) from L3-L5 and 70% of a disk. I may have to have further surgeries to replace the disk that was mostly removed.

....

Larry
xxxx Engineer
xxxx Corporation

Mark Craythorn <markcraythorn@hotmail.com>
06/26/2007 01:10 PM

To: <Larry@xxxxx.com>

Subject: RE: Hi Larry

Yikes!!!!

Sounds very painful. I'll keep you in my prayers.
Hopefully they can fix you up better than you were before.

Best Regards
~Mark

And the outcome at least at the time of writing did seem positive:

To: markcraythorn@htmail.com
Subject: RE: Hi Larry
From: Larry@xxxxx.com
Date: Wed, 27 Jun 2007 11:04:18 – 0400

Well, I can now feel my feet. Recovery will take some time but the short term outcome seems positive. I'll have to have the disk replaced; it's a matter of time.

Larry
XXXX Engineer
XXXX Corporation

By the time I got around to writing this all down in February 2008 Larry had still not needed any further surgery. He is missing one disk, without a fusion. Particularly remarkable is that he has been walking without a cane for eight months. Also for the past six months he only needed to take medication for this condition on three occasions; and one of them was when he moved a 500lb wood furnace into his basement!

All of this shows that we need to pray about everything and we especially need to ask God to heal us. God does hear our prayers and has the ability to heal us instantly, yet this is often not his way. His answers may not always come in the timeframe that we expect them to and may not come in the ways that we expect them to. His ways are beyond ours. They cause us to dig deep inside us and to grow as people. He is preparing us for eternity with Him. He is going to do the job right.

12. *God and losing someone you love*

I learned a lot about how to hear the voice of God from Raymond. In all likelihood Raymond is not someone who you have ever heard of. That in no way diminishes his greatness before God who uses the humble, people of this world to do great things.

Raymond had been a pastor of a church in Texas where I met him, and had afterwards moved for a brief time to Ireland as a missionary, returning eventually to Texas due to sickness. It was with great sadness that I heard of Raymond's eventual passing away from Parkinson's disease. He left behind a wife, Marie, and teenage daughter Shelby.

Friends and relatives initially rallied around Marie, but after time, they got on with their own lives leaving Marie to cope alone. One day things were particularly bad for her as she battled with her thoughts. She still needed comfort, yet God who sees everything knew in His wisdom what Marie needed that day. She needed to know that someone cared. God knew that. He prompted me to send Marie a simple message:

From: "Mark Craythorn" <markcraythorn@hotmail.com>
To: Marie@xxxxx.com
Subject: The Lord is with you and loves you deeply
Date: Sat, 23 Sep 2006 20:40:38 -0400

Marie,

The Lord wants you to know that he is with you. He sees everything and nothing escapes His attention. Right now He is very interested in the things going on in your life.

Bless you
In Christ
~Mark

God and email.

And Marie responded with:

From: Marie@xxxxx.com
To: markcraythorn@hotmail.com
Subject: RE: The Lord is with you and loves you deeply
Date: Sun, 24 Sep 2006 03:37:37 +0000

Dear Mark,

Thank you so much for that. I have been so down lately. I really miss Raymond and feel like I have been left alone again. I know it is the enemy but it is hard to get past some things. Thank you! It is good to hear a word from the Lord.

Please give my regards to Lisa.

God bless you and your family,
Marie

God knows when we are feeling down. He knows the pain that we go through when someone we love dies. He wants to be there to help us through this difficult time. We do well to remember the words of Jesus: "Unless a grain of wheat falls into the ground and dies, it remains alone; but if it dies, it produces much grain."

God's ways are beyond ours. He always has both our utmost good and eternity in mind. If we and our loved ones walk in His ways and trust in Him then we will see our loved ones again beyond the grave. This is the hope we have as Christians.

13.   *God gives us hope*

But God is still not finished with Marie and Shelby who I wrote about in the last chapter. God is still trying to bring comfort to them. Their family is still hurting. He knows that it takes us a long, long time to get past the worst grief of losing a loved one and He is with us all through the grieving process. Four months after the message in the last chapter God gave me a powerful prophetic dream about Raymond, her husband who had passed away:

Mark Craythorn <markcraythorn@hotmail.com
To: Marie@xxxxx.com
Subject: What's up?
Date: Tue, 1 May 2007 10:38:54 -0400

Hi Marie,

The Lord gave me a really powerful dream last night. In it I saw Raymond. He was different somehow, older, greyer, whiter but in a radiant way. There were a group of people near an intersection waiting, expecting him. He stepped out from the crowd into the street, paced up and down the center of the street proclaiming and declaring the kingdom of God. I saw people begin to worship God right there in the street.
....
Then I was in a building and the congregation was going to pray for you and Raymond as you were going out to the mission field. I heard Shelby say "what about me, don't forget to pray for me". So they prayed for all of you.

So what does this mean?

There must be something going on in your life right now that the Lord is interested in. I find that Raymond walked the center of the road - a good place to be. I see that he was

---

not deterred by others (the traffic around him). I see that he
has been changed/transformed by the Lord. I see that he
continues to impact lives.

....

And I also found it interesting that the Lord still considers
you all family: husband and wife together, those whom the
Lord has joined together. There is more about Shelby but I
wanted to first ask you what is going on in her life that you
think may have caused the Lord to focus his attention on
her? But it was a very powerful dream for me, more so
than my usual prophetic dreams so I know that God is
really really involved in what is going on.

So of course I am curious.

Blessings in Christ
~Mark

Marie replied that she had been thinking of moving to the
Philippines in two years time to work with a Children's Home
there. She also said that her daughter Shelby had "just last
week" heard about a Christian missions organization called
Youth With A Mission (YWAM) that runs a Discipleship
Training School (DTS) with a missions outreach into Russia,
a country she has been interested in "since she was fairly
young". Shelby had also been having problems dealing with
the passing of her father.

From: Marie@xxxxx.com
To: markcraythorn@hotmail.com
Subject: RE: What's up?
Date: Tue, 1 May 2007 15:05:45 +0000

Hello Mark,

Wow! What an awesome dream! There are several things
going on in our life at the moment. I have been thinking
that I will move to the Philippines in 2 years when Shelby
will be graduating. Things have really taken off there in
regards to a Children's Home that the Lord had spoken to

> me about back in 2004. In the mean time...Shelby, since she was fairly young has felt that she was to go to Russia. Just last week we have heard of YWAM's DTS program with the target country being Russia. She is absolutely thrilled with the prospect. Shelby has had some problems dealing with Raymond's death and the fact that we are not a family any more.
>
> ....
>
> I too am curious about this all. What do you think? This is so precious to me.
> Marie

Marie still has God firmly in her sights even after the grief of losing her husband. God still has great plans for her. God also has great plans for her daughter Shelby.

> From: Mark Craythorn <markcraythorn@hotmail.com>
> To: Marie <Marie@xxxxx.com>
> Subject: RE: What's up?
> Date: Tue, 1 May 2007 23:16:57 -0400
>
> Hi Marie,
>
> Wow awesome stuff going on in your lives, so:
>
> As far as the children's home goes I think that is definitely something that the Lord would bless. I think that He is confirming along the way.
>
> As far as Shelby is concerned, the Lord IS DEFINITELY confirming her calling too!!!!!!!! I find it interesting that my family was also part of YWAM and the Lord called us very very clearly when He called us to them. They have a great program for someone like Shelby just coming out of school. Where is this DTS located? It would be just like the Lord to connect all the dots and send her where her heart is. It is very significant that this is happening just after you found out about the DTS with the outreach to Russia.

God and email.

An intersection in a dream also means a place of decision; a making up of one's mind. You could go one way or the other. Neither way is of itself "wrong" and the Lord will bless either way. The Lord loves you so much He simply says "you choose", go where you want and I will bless it.

Note that in my dream Shelby asked "what about me". The congregation prayed for her to go out on the mission field as well. The Lord is confirming His call on her life. Please show her this email that she might know even more clearly in her heart that the Lord is calling and confirming. He does that with those He loves. She needs to know this from someone other than her mother. She needs to know that it is not just something that she grew up into because she is a part of your family, but that it is a clear and separate call from the Lord on her life. She obviously has her own relationship with the Lord and has touched His heart.

Also for Shelby she needs to know that Raymond continues to look down upon her from heaven and that she will walk in his legacy. A pretty good place to be if you ask me. She is blessed to have had him go before her. The Lord still considers the 3 of you as family. If we fix our eyes on eternity we see that those that pass on from this world are really still with us. Nothing, not even death, can take that unity away from us.

. . . .

Blessings in Christ
~Mark

God knew that Shelby was feeling left out and was asking inside herself, "God, what about me? Do you really care for me? Am I really called to be a worker in your Kingdom?" God reads our hearts, He gave us a picture of the congregation in the dream praying for Shelby thereby confirming that He heard the heart cry of this teenager and confirming His call on her life.

Raymond laid some incredible groundwork in the lives of both Marie and Shelby. Both mother and daughter are going to continue the legacy left by Raymond. What an amazing legacy to step into! As a teenager who is going against the prevailing culture, and trying to lead a life that follows Christ, Shelby needed to know that God was still with her. Who better to confirm that in her life than God Himself?

Their reaction to that email was:

From: Marie@xxxxx.com
To: markcraythorn@hotmail.com
Subject: RE: What's up?
Date: Thu, 3 May 2007 15:30:38 +0000

Hi Mark,

We have had a breakthrough! When I read the e-mail to Shelby (actually we read it together!) we were both just weeping because of the goodness of the Lord. Shelby is ecstatic! For so long now she has felt like the weird one in school because of her desires. This is such a confirmation <of her calling from God>.
….

So with that said...our lives have been changed because of your dream. We really needed to hear from the Lord. Thank you so much for sharing with us. You have been a blessing.

Please give Lisa my best regards,
Marie

By pointing ahead to the future and encouraging them, God was showing them the great things that He still has in store for both of them. Knowing that God is behind us can give us the courage and strength to continue in the face of losing a loved one.

God and email.

We need to remember that the Lord provides comfort for us when we grieve the loss of our loved ones. If anyone can do anything for us at that time it will be Him. This alone is a powerful reason for anyone to stay close to God. Wouldn't you like to know that the Creator of the Universe is close to you after you have lost a loved one?

14.   *God looks after our children.*

As we saw in the last chapter, when we choose to stay close to God He looks after our children too. He wants to give our children faith to believe that He will do great and marvelous things in their lives.

As parents we are concerned about our children. God wants to allay those fears. He is ultimately the one that is concerned for them even more than we are.

Annie lives in Houston Texas with her husband Peter and two daughters, Amanda and Betty, the oldest who is a young teenager. The children attend a Christian school and the entire family has a solid Christian faith.

> From: Mark Craythorn
> [mailto:markcraythorn@hotmail.com]
> Sent: Saturday, April 21, 2007 8:37 PM
> To: Annie@xxxxx.com
> Subject: God with you
>
> Hi Annie,
>
> Just wanted to let you know that over the past few days I really felt that God wants you to know that He is with you.
>
> God Bless
> ~Mark

Annie knew why God was very close to her; it was because of her daughter Betty.

> RE: God with you
>
> From: Annie (Annie@xxxxx.com)

God and email.

Sent: Sun 4/22/07 12:27 AM

To: 'Mark Craythorn' (markcraythorn@hotmail.com)

Hi Mark,

Thank you for the beautiful message. I, too, have felt God's strong presence these past few days as I wrestle with parenting issues. I don't think we grow as parents in small, graduated steps but rather by fits and starts with some cataclysmic upheavals thrown in. I am in the midst of one of those cataclysmic upheavals that has stretched me well past my knowledge base.

Betty is in the process of moving from the 'faith of her parents' to making it her own. Although this is what we fervently pray happens for our children, the search can be hard for child and parent alike. She so desperately wants to feel God and to hear His voice. She feels like her prayers are "talking to herself" and that she doesn't ever feel the presence of the Holy Spirit in her life. She is truly putting her heart into her search for Him; she gets up at 6am every morning for her devotions and voraciously reads all manner of materials relating to Christianity. Her questions are deep and many times are beyond my capacity to answer them. A wonderful Christian counselor is helping guide her (and me) in finding some of these answers and she is warming to the idea of talking to her youth pastor. (An exasperating facet of teenagers is their unwillingness to open up to others for fear of embarrassment).

God led me to a seminar today given by <name withheld>. I alternated between tears, goosebumps, and elation as what I heard affirmed my efforts and gave me huge insights into the next steps I am to take. I have no doubt as to the outcome of all this; Betty will always be a great warrior for Jesus. I would like to ask for your prayers for Betty as she seeks a personal relationship with God and for His wisdom for us as parents.

We think of you and your sweet family so often and miss you all terribly! Please say hello to Lisa for me!

God's Blessings,

Annie

Annie summed it up very nicely. God had led her that very day to a seminar that had addressed her concerns as a parent. God was showing Annie that the message that she had heard at the seminar was a good message, one that He approved of. God was whispering to Annie that it was all going to be ok as her daughter Betty struggled to make her faith "her own" and move beyond the "faith of her parents".

God is not intimidated by our doubt in His existence or His ultimate goodness. He is patient with us and draws us slowly to Him. Betty is in the process of making Christ her own as we all ultimately must.

We all need to investigate this Jesus, this Christ and the claims He makes. If we draw near to Christ with honest answers, and a desire to know the truth, then he will not turn us away empty handed. It requires a patience and readiness to wait on God for the answers. In the end we will obtain the knowledge that we seek, and having found that truth we find in turn that it has set us free.

15. God comforts

You may think that God is especially close to those involved in full time "ministry". That might be partly true, but those in ministry usually take time to be with God in prayer; they want to know that what they are doing aligns with God's agenda. It is prayer that unlocks the keys to the things of God. Perhaps you need to hear how God has worked in the life of someone who is not a missionary, minister or pastor.

Beth who lives in Texas also spends time with God in prayer. She is not in regular full time ministry. She is a stay at home mom, a wife and mother to two grown children, one who has just finished college and another who has just finished high school. What sets Beth apart is that she loves God with all her heart.

But a crisis can rock even those who love God: something was due to come undone in Beth's world. Unbeknownst to both Beth & I, someone set in motion vicious accusations against Beth on May 8, the day that I sent this email, and Beth & I were still blissfully unaware of it.

From: markcraythorn@hotmail.com
To: Beth@xxxxx.com
Subject: God with you
Date: Tue, 8 May 2007 08:54:05 -0400

Hi Beth,

Wanted to tell you that God is showing me that He is really with you right now.

God Bless
~Mark

Upon receiving this email the crisis was yet to unfold in Beth's life so her reply to me indicated that she still didn't grasp the fact of just how close God had drawn to her. But God already knew what was going to happen. He was preparing her for what was coming later that day, and assuring her that He was on her side, and that He would continue to walk with her through it. She would need to see God walking through the crisis with her and to know that He was on her side.

I only came to know of some of the details of the accusation thirteen days later. Without going into the details of the situation, I could look back after the crisis had run its course and see that God had been preparing Beth. He had walked through this alongside her. While I had told Beth that God was going to be with her, she needed to be reminded again so that she could see that fact again for herself. So I followed up with another email:

> FW: God with you
> From: Mark Craythorn (markcraythorn@hotmail.com)
> Sent: Mon 5/21/07 8:51 AM
> To: Beth@xxxxx.com
>
> Hi Beth,
> … If you say that "2 weeks ago <this incident happened then> that puts it at the time I sent this email <above>. Since I am not regularly in the habit of emailing you I think that you can easily see that God already knew what was happening & He is showing you that He is behind you 100%.
>
> Have a blessed week.
> ~Mark

Now Beth understood:

> Re: FW: God with you
> From: Beth@xxxxx.com
> Sent: Mon 5/21/07 9:03 AM
> To: markcraythorn@hotmail.com

> OH MY GOSH.. YOU ARE SO RIGHT MARK...
> THANKS YOU SO MUCH.. I REALLY NEEDED THAT
> TODAY.... ITS A HARD DAY...
> BETH

"OH MY GOSH", it was clear as daylight now - God had been with her all the time.

There is a very real devil out there and he opposes the people of God and the things of God. We need to stand against him and God in His wisdom will bring us through. God gives us strength to stand against whatever the enemy throws at us and will even bring good out of the situation ensuring that we come out the trial "refined" like gold.

There is a strength and peace of spirit that God gives to followers of Christ that cannot be shattered by anything that the world throws at them. It is the type of strength that can cause one to lay down his life for a child, for his brother or sister, or for a friend. It is the type of strength that Jesus displayed on the cross when He laid down His life for us.

16.   *God and those going on a journey*

There is no place that we can travel to that is beyond the orbit of God's care. God has shown me on numerous occasions that He takes additional steps to place our lives under His special protection when we journey away from home. It is important for us to know that He is looking after us wherever we go in this world.

While I was in Hong Kong on a business trip God showed me in a dream that Colin, a friend of mine, working as a computer professional in South Africa, was also going on a trip.

From: Mark Craythorn
[mailto:markcraythorn@hotmail.com]
Sent: 10 October 2006 23:54
To: Colin@xxxxx.com
Subject: Stuff

Hi Colin,

I had a dream about you last night that I believe came from God and He gave it to me because He is trying to show you that He is with you in a stronger way than usual at this time. In the dream you were studying something. Also you were going to go somewhere.

So now I am curious. What's up? What's going on right now?

On my side this is being written from Hong Kong. I am on a business trip ….

That's it for now.
God Bless
~Mark

God and email.

Colin confirmed that he was in fact going to go on a trip. There was a lot more going on in his life as well:

From: Colin@xxxxx.com
To: markcraythorn@hotmail.com
Subject: RE: Stuff
Date: Wed, 11 Oct 2006 10:59:55 +0200

Hi Mark

Good to hear from you. Sounds like you are having an awesome time.

2006 has been one of our toughest years, mainly due to a lack of sleep. Our boy has been quite sick over the past 8 months, and has not slept well. He wakes up 2-3 times a night, so we probably average around 4 hours sleep. This has affected us in that we are both pretty tired, battle to spend quality time with the Lord and each other. On top of that, work has been busy. I have taken on more of a management role over and above my technical responsibilities. This has been quite a challenge. Sheryl's business has been quite stressful, as a number of training opportunities aborted at the 99th hour. As a result, her cashflow is a huge problem. We are just trusting God to provide there.

As to your questions, I'm about to leave for Swaziland on a business trip for a couple of days. Also, we are leading a group at the church responsible for overhauling the cell groups in the church. We felt the approach was to pray and wait on the Lord to show us the way. He is so faithful, and we are making headway, as we form the plan 1 step at a time. This could be the "studying" side, as we are seeking the Lord for the way forward.

Well, must go.
Lots of Love to Lisa and the Kids.

Cheers

God and email.

Colin.

Colin was leaving for Swaziland, a country adjoining South Africa, on a business trip in a few days time. Colin was stressed and tired, his son was sick and his wife Sheryl was also under pressure.

It was no wonder God wanted to show Colin that He would be with him on the trip. It also showed that since God knew about this trip, this one detail in Colin's life, that it was obvious that He knew about all of the other things as well and would take care of Colin's family in his absence.

As for spending "quality time with the Lord", God knew where Colin's heart was, Colin's heart was with God and that was all that counted.

17.   *God when we are tired and weary*

My wife Lisa and I relocated our family from South Africa to the USA many years ago but the ties that bind us to South Africa remain strong. We have family there and also try as best as we can, given the distance, to maintain some friendships there. Once in the US we moved around a lot as I traveled for business. We lived in various states but finally settled in Ohio and now it seems like a lifetime since we ever lived in South Africa. Nevertheless, despite the distance we still try to maintain contact by visiting every few years and emailing family and friends there from time to time.

John does not attend church but I have seen a lot of evidence of God being with John over the years.

At the exact time I wrote from Hong Kong to Colin (from the prior chapter) about his impending business trip to Swaziland, John was also on a business trip to Swaziland. I had no idea that John was there but God did and He gave me a dream that John was feeling depressed but that God cared and was watching over John wanting to help him feel better.

From: Mark Craythorn
[mailto:markcraythorn@hotmail.com]
Sent: 10 October 2006 06:19 AM
To: John
Subject: How are you

Hey John,

God is watching over you dude. What's up you feeling a bit down lately?

I told Lisa that I was feeling this way and she told me that she had been thinking about you a lot lately so that confirmed it for me; hence this email.

God and email.

> So here is what you need to hear...
> Sometimes the things in life get us down but on the flip side: You have an incredible family. The kids love their mom & dad loads. Work on loving Sue & you will find that what goes around comes around. Then as far as the more extended family is concerned, if you step back and look at the details you will find God at work in that too and when he is involved there then that is ALWAYS a good thing. Expect things to improve. You will see that things will get better.
>
> Bless you
> ~Mark

John appreciated the email and confirmed on his return from Swaziland that the stresses of life had been getting to him:

> Subject: RE: How are you
> Date: Fri, 13 Oct 2006 11:03:22 +0200
> From: John@xxxxx.com
> To: markcraythorn@hotmail.com
>
> Hello
>
> Thanks for the mail Mark, I appreciated it. Yeah things have been getting a bit rough again, maybe I've been a bit too negative again or something like that, I'm just tired. A lot of the time it's a battle at work, it's a battle at home, it's a personal battle and then there is not much rest. I'm not going into all the details, but I've been extremely unhappy lately with my job, my marriage, my personal growth, the status of this country, the cost of everything, the financial battle to live an "acceptable" life style for my family, interest rate hikes happening again (gone up 1.5% already, going up another 0.5 in December, and the trend will continue next year, currently on 12%, has hit us hard, my bond and car repayments have increased by about R1000 a month since the start of the hikes, with no salary increase this year, as in 0% increase).

God and email.

Anyway, thanks for the prayers and the thoughts, I'll be alright, just need to get through it all again, consolidate, filter out the unimportant, concentrate on the important and hope that the rest just follows.

Sorry for only replying now, I was in Swaziland on business.

Love and miss all of you.
Cheers
John

xxxxxx | xxxxx Systems | John
John@xxxxx.com

As I mentioned before John doesn't attend church except on rare occasions yet despite this God was clearly calling to John and trying to pull Him out of his depression. It should show us clearly that church attendance is not a prerequisite for us being able to go to God and lay our struggles before Him. Quite the contrary, in fact God in His mercy is concerned about our struggles and wants to alleviate the pain associated with them. All He is waiting for is for us to ask Him to do so.

What we need to realize is that all that is required from us is that we come to God in prayer. We come *just as we are* asking Him to help us.

"Come to me all you who are heavy laden and I will give you rest", promises Jesus. These promises echo down the hallways of time and are still as relevant today as they were 2000 years ago.

18.   *God gives mothers strength*

Vicki and her husband Chris have done full time missions work in Africa with Youth With A Mission's Mercy Ships. Volunteers on these ships visit difficult to reach areas of the world bringing much needed doctors, surgery rooms, medical supplies and clinics to people that have no access to expert medical care or are unable to afford the expense of complicated medical procedures.
(for more information see http://www.mercyships.org).

Vicky and Chris' family had expanded during their time on the ship to include two children and they had eventually relocated from their home base in the United Kingdom to Tyler Texas in the USA. I had not emailed or spoken to them in a few months but God knew that Vicki was trying to make a decision:

From: Mark Craythorn
[mailto:markcraythorn@hotmail.com]
Sent: 12 May 2007 05:53
To: vicki@xxxxx.com
Subject: Trust

Vicki,

I hear the Lord saying this to you today: "Trust in the Lord your God with all your heart and lean not on your own understanding. In all your ways acknowledge Him and He will direct your path".

God Bless
~Mark

Vicki knew what this was about:

RE: Trust

From: Vicki (vicki@xxxxx.com)
Sent: Mon 5/14/07 10:26 AM
To: 'Mark Craythorn' (markcraythorn@hotmail.com)

Thanks Mark!
That's one of my 'life verses'
I guess I have been wondering whether I should continue to be a stay at home Mom or start work when Beka turns 3. Perhaps that is the Lord telling me that He hears and will guide...
Love Vicki

God knew how to touch Vicki. By touching on one of her "life verses", God was showing her how much He knew her. God was telling Vicki that if she would embrace her "life verse" then He would impart His wisdom to her and she would end up making the right decision for her daughter Beka and herself. She was able to rest in the assurance that God himself would guide and that His wisdom is infallible.

I think that by now you will be starting to see that God doesn't concern Himself so much about what we do as He concerns Himself about the state of our well-being. He wants us to experience love, peace and joy and to live our lives in a way that reflects that.

If you try to stay close to God and follow in His ways then God will impart similar wisdom to you in your decision making. Even if you are unaware that you are being guided from within by God, God can still impart His thoughts on a matter to you, helping you to make right decisions. That is not to say that you will be immune from making incorrect decisions, but just that are chances of doing so are greatly diminished, and where you do make incorrect decisions God will give you new opportunities to correct them. Having this knowledge will free you from worry and anxiety and permit you to walk confidently and securely through life.

19.   *God loves families*

My family lives in the USA and my extended family lives in South Africa. I have lived and worked on multiple continents and because of this most of the families that I have written about in this book are scattered all over the map. I really have no idea what is going on in the day to day activities of their lives but God loves these families deeply and is very involved in their lives.

But even when God is at work in our lives, He respects our privacy and doesn't broadcast our problems and needs for all and sundry to hear. Often when He asks me to contact someone He omits some of the details, leaving it up to that person to decide whether or not they want to open up and share the intimate things of their lives with me.

Sometimes when God asks me to contact someone it can be puzzling for me not knowing the full details for the reasons behind the request. God gives us the first step and asks us to take that step in faith trusting in Him to work out the rest of the details.

I also find that when I know what is happening in the day to day lives of people it influences how I hear from God and sometimes it can even be a hindrance. I need to be careful not to take what I have heard from God and add my knowledge to it because God may be speaking about something that is totally unrelated to anything I know about that person and I will be of no help to the person if I allow my thoughts to cloud the situation.

I live in the same city as Chris and we attend the same church. He is the executive pastor and is often to be found leading a "Holy Spirit" weekend retreat. I sent this email to Chris:

God and email.

> From: markcraythorn@hotmail.com
> Sent: Monday, October 30, 2006 10:42 AM
> To: Chris
> Subject: Hi Chris
>
> Hi Chris,
>
> I felt very strongly towards the end of last week that the
> Lord was with you more than usual and then I realized that
> you have the Holy Spirit weekend coming up this coming
> weekend - so I guess it is probably Him being in the
> planning that goes into that. Should be a good weekend.
>
> Have a good week.
> Blessings
> ~Mark

But although God was involved in that "Holy Spirit " retreat,
God was far more interested in the personal details of Chris'
life. Chris shared some of what he had been doing with me.
He had taken a day off work to be with his wife Lindy that
Friday:

> " Chris" <Chris@xxxxx.com>
> 11/01/2006 01:40 PM
>
> Mark: Thanks…, I took a day of vacation last Friday to
> spend with Lindy. Our lives have been so hectic with the
> opening of the Community Center and other affairs going
> on at the church that we needed the time to connect. We
> had a nice day together doing nothing, and your word was
> confirmation that the Lord placed value on it as well.
>
> Blessings. Chris.

And minutes later Chris remembered that he had also
preached at his grand-baby's church the Sunday that she had
been dedicated to the Lord:

From: "Chris" <Chris@xxxxx.com>
Sent: 11/01/2006
To:markcraythorn@hotmail.com
Subject: RE: Hi Chris

Mark: Thanks….. I also had the opportunity to preach at
my daughter Joy's Vineyard <Church> this last Sunday
during which my grand-baby Naomi was dedicated. It was
a great time, and I had the opportunity to <share the
message of Jesus with someone close> at the reception.
All in all, a good weekend. Thanks for keeping me in your
thoughts and prayers. God is good.

Blessings. Chris.

Time with his wife and also the dedication of his grand-baby
to the Lord; these were all family activities that Chris had
been involved in. Chris had told me what he had been doing
but I wanted to be sure that Chris had seen the same thing
that I had seen. Sometimes when we are in the midst of the
busyness of our lives we can't see the forest for the trees. I
wanted to make sure that Chris knew exactly what God was
trying to show him:

From:
markcraythorn@hotmail.com[mailto:mark.craythorn@hot
mail.com]
Sent: Wednesday, November 01, 2006
To: Chris
Subject: RE: Hi Chris

Chris,

So God was indeed at work. I am going to venture to say
that the Lord was working strongly in your preparation of
last Sunday's message. He wants you to know that He sees
everything you do. He is pleased with you. In addition to
that He wants to show you just how much He loves your
family and how much He loves Naomi - that is very, very

evident. She is going to be used of the Lord in the future.

Yes the upcoming weekend will be good but based on what you replied it is immediately evident to me that your family is probably the most important reason why the Lord is speaking: the things that are closer and more intimate to you - spending time with family - are of special importance to the Lord. He wants you to know that He sees the intimate things of your life and He places a high value on them.

Be blessed today
~Mark

First the special day with his wife, and second the baptism of his grand-baby with the family in attendance. It had been a family orientated weekend for Chris. God was confirming to Chris that the entire family, husbands, wives, parents, grandparents, children, and even all the relatives have a special place in the heart of God.

God especially enjoyed the fact that Chris took time off from his busy schedule at the church just to be with his wife. Prioritizing his wife over work moved the heart of God. God loves families, and He loves marriage too. Why else do we begin married life in church before God? It was Him who instituted marriage after all. God wanted to affirm Chris in what he had done. Who wouldn't want God's affirmation?

Chris had preached that weekend and that for him was "work". It was something that he was often called upon to do in his role of executive pastor in the church. This work that he does is important to God but families are even more important to God, so when Chris was involved in the baby dedication with his family in attendance, it pleased the heart of God and God wanted Chris to know that.

This should be a continual reminder to us that we need to be spending time with our families. And when we are blessed to be able to spend time with them we must just relax and enjoy them for who they are; love them unconditionally. God does. Who are we to do otherwise?

The story of God being close to this family continued later:

From: Mark Craythorn
[mailto:markcraythorn@hotmail.com]
Sent: Friday, February 15, 2008 9:02 AM
To: Chris
Subject: God with you

 Hi Chris,

… your son … God is telling me that He is with him now…

Now I have no idea what situation he finds himself in but I do know that this is what the Lord is saying to him. The Lord very is close to him now. Please pass this on to him.

Blessings in Christ
~Mark

This time God's closeness was related to Chris' son and his wife. I didn't know that his wife was pregnant but God did:

RE: God with you
From: Chris (Chris@xxxx.org)
Sent: Thu 3/13/08 2:13 PM
To: Mark Craythorn (markcraythorn@hotmail.com)

Mark:
Sorry for not returning a reply more promptly. I've passed it on to …, my son. You might be interested to know that he and his wife Emma just had their 2nd child … last week. All of them …. are doing very well….. At the time (of your email) Emma was in the 3rd week of enforced bed rest after a close call with premature labor 6 weeks before her due date. We … were all scrambling to assist in caring for their two year old. Though they were taking the

challenge in good spirits, I know that the bed rest was wearing thin.

Thanks, as always....

Blessings,

Chris.

God is with us when we go through the good times and the difficult times. Just as we need to be spending time with our families in the good times, we need to come alongside them and support them when they go through difficult times.

Note that God did not remove this burden from the family. Chris clearly said that they "were all scrambling to assist in caring for their two year old". God allowed the stressful situation to become a catalyst for everyone to rally around and support each other and God was also showing that He knew about and was involved in the situation. Normally we pray for God to spare us from difficult times but in this case God used a difficult situation to help a family draw even closer to each other and to demonstrate His knowledge of events. Surely God's ways are higher than our ways.

20.   *God has more than one message*

From the previous real life accounts of God at work in people's lives you might have noticed that God often is doing more than one thing in our lives. We often try to compartmentalize our lives. We act one way at school, another way at work, another way in front of our families and reserve our most proper behavior for church activities. But God doesn't see us in that way at all. He wants to be involved in ALL areas of our lives. It follows that when He speaks to us, we need to be careful to listen correctly so that we hear all that He is trying to tell us.

I have previously mentioned William, who is a pastor friend of mine, living near Boston with his wife Pam and two children. God showed me two things about William, firstly that God was with him on a particular day and secondly that William had hidden deep inside him a desire to teach. So the next day I sent William this email:

> From: Mark Craythorn
> [mailto:markcraythorn@hotmail.com]
> Sent: Tuesday, May 15, 2007 7:34 AM
> To: William@xxxxx.com
> Subject: Hi
>
> Hi William,
>
> Well what are you up to now? God is showing me that He is really with you right now. It is related to wanting to teach something. So I was wondering what you are up to.
>
> God Bless
> ~Mark

God and email.

While God only shared with me a few things going on in William's life, it immediately became apparent that there was a whole lot else going on as well:

From: William@xxxxxx.com
To: markcraythorn@hotmail.com
Subject: RE: Hi
Date: Tue, 15 May 2007 13:43:21 -0400

Hi Mark,

.... a few things are going on.

I do sense God calling me (back? further?) into intimacy with him.
.....

we just moved out of our house yesterday because we are adding a second floor, and ripping up the first floor, and almost completely rebuilding the house. I thought it would have been cheaper to move into a bigger house, and normally it probably would have been, but I think God is up to something else. Have a Christian builder, who is doing a great job. He said to me this morning: "You must have a connection up there." Because he has received three separate loads of cement, all free, from deliveries that were done in my area and had leftovers. Totalled only maybe $1000 in savings, but was the "coincidence" of the timing, three different days, just happened to be a truck each time he called, with just enough left over for three separate pourings.

I think God is teaching me and Pam his provision. And just this morning I was struck with a "crazy" prayer, one of those God-sized prayers, that our house would be completely done, inside and out, without us running out of the money we got from refinancing, or having to borrow more. I know the numbers, and this is not feasible. But I know God, and I sensed maybe that is how I am supposed to pray. So that's what I am going to do!

I am heading to Maine at the end of the month for 5 days and 4 nights alone in with God. That's about all the big news from here! Thanks for praying for me.

What's up with you?

Blessings,
Will

The timing of the email was very interesting. It happened at the time William moved his wife Pam and their two children out of their house so that it could undergo some major reconstruction. God was trying to show William that He would be with their family during that difficult time.

Even the builder recognized that there was something going on when he received three "free" loads of cement. He recognized that William had "a connection up there" in heaven. God was busy orchestrating things in all areas of William's life.

But I was still puzzled about the teaching/students/university so I had to ask about that too:

From: Mark Craythorn
[mailto:markcraythorn@hotmail.com]
Sent: Tuesday, May 15, 2007 5:22 PM
To: William
Subject: RE: Hi

Hi William,

…..

What I have found is that when God speaks it is usually related to present circumstances: so that being said, and since you moved out of your house yesterday, I do think that God is showing you that He is in your house construction process AND that He heard your prayer this morning. So it would not surprise me if He would do what you asked so that your "*house would be completely done, inside and out, without us running out of the money we got from refinancing, or having to borrow more*".

I also think He delights in showing you that He cares for you whether or not you spend time with Him.

....

And then I need to ask if you are involved with anything related to students/university??

God Bless
~Mark

God knows all things about us. There is nothing that we can keep from Him. William's reply confirmed that God had seen into the deepest recesses of his heart. God had seen William's passion.

RE: Hi
From: William (William@xxxxxx.com)
Sent: Wed 5/16/07 8:53 AM
To: 'Mark Craythorn' (markcraythorn@hotmail.com)

....

I am not currently involved with students/university. .... It is still my passion. It has come to Rob in his prayers for me, too, recently. Rob and I recently talked about me someday moving to Boston and starting a (Church) satellite aimed at college students. Pam was open to it.

Part of me also wants to go overseas. Not necessarily with a missions organization, but as a tent-maker, maybe getting certified to teach English as a second language, moving to Africa, or Latin America, or Asia, with Pam and I working secular jobs and letting the Spirit use us as missionaries.

Rob is the senior pastor of William's church. When the senior pastor and a Godly friend both hear God saying the same things about your deepest hidden desires, then you can be sure that it is God that has seen those desires. He will continue to awaken those desires, training and maturing William to have the confidence to bring his desires to full fruition in God's own perfect time.

William is still feeling out how this might happen. He is thinking about possibly starting an extension of his existing church aimed at college students. He is also thinking about teaching English as a second language overseas. It may be one of these things, it may be both that come to pass in the end. God will give William clarity and enable him to make the correct decisions when the time is right. For now it is sufficient to know that God sees this desire of William's. Isn't it amazing to know that God can see into our hearts like that?

God knows all of the details of your life too. He sees all of your struggles, and frustrations, but if you let Him into your life, and live a life centered on Him, He will be in there with you too, championing your cause and celebrating your successes every step of your journey.

Would you like God to be there for you on the journey of your life as well? Would you like the assurance that the creator of the universe is behind you? If so, there is more on that for you in the next chapter.

21.   *The God decision*

Up until now you may have been reading this, finding it interesting but not really thinking about how you can apply it in your own life. I want to assure you that if God can talk to me in my life then He can certainly do it in yours as well. I can tell you how to experience this conversational relationship with God if you want that for yourself.

God wants to initiate this relationship with you now. No rules, no expectations, no preconditions. Just you and Him as you are right now. You don't have to change a thing about who you are at this point. Just come to Him as you are.

You need to accept that God is very real. You need to accept that the claims of Christianity are true; that Jesus is the very Son of God and that He chose to die for your sins. You need to turn your back on your past sinful ways choosing instead to follow Jesus and His teachings. If you sincerely want to do this, and you desire this rich relationship with God that you see spoken of in this book, your life will be transformed forever. God Himself will see to it.

If you want this relationship with God then read through this prayer below once and afterwards pray it to Him. As you pray, believe what you are saying and pray it to God with all of your heart:

Father in Heaven, I confess that I am a sinner. I have not always walked in your ways, I believe in Jesus as much as I am able to at this point. Help me in areas where I still struggle with my unbelief and strengthen my belief in you. I choose to believe that Jesus Christ died for me, that He rose from the dead and that He has taken away my sins. Please cleanse me, make me new and fill me with your Holy Spirit.
Amen.

If you did that then you have become "born again" and God's Holy Spirit has come to live in you and be your guide.

The book of Mark from the Bible is included in the Appendix at the end of this book. You will be given new eyes and understanding to read it and will find it more alive than ever before. Strive to understand it and God will reward you.

Then just begin to talk to God. Talk to Him any time you want. Prayer is simply conversation with God. Tell him your doubts, your struggles, tell him about the blessings He has given you and how much you appreciate them. Be intentional and set aside time each day to be with God. Also take some time at the end just to be quiet and to listen to Him speaking back to you through your thoughts. And be patient, a good relationship takes time to develop. You will begin to recognize the voice of God more and more as you take time to be with Him.

22. *God will talk to you too*

God can use other people to talk into your life. These can be and most often are the people closest to you. They are usually people that you trust since you will be more inclined to listen to them. But God is not limited in speaking to you only through these people, occasionally God will even speak into your life from an unexpected source.

Dan, who is one of the pastors at the church I attend, shared a recent time in his life where God used Him to speak words of encouragement to a lady that he came across at a rental car agency:

Subject: hello!
Date: Thu, 5 Apr 2007 16:26:57 -0400
From: Dan@xxxxx.com
To: markcraythorn@hotmail.com

Hi Mark,

It was really good having lunch with you. The prophetic words that you shared with me were meaningful. Oddly enough, I traveled to Boston a few days later and would end up having prophetic words for a lady who worked at the rental car agency I rented my car from. You reinvigorated my awareness of God's present voice in those situations. The lady was crying and deeply encouraged and I am having more anticipation of such encounters.

Warmly in Christ,

Dan

If you come away from an encounter with someone invigorated and renewed and more aware of the presence of

God in your life then you can be sure that God was involved in it somewhere. This was definitely the case with both Dan and the woman at the rental car agency.

If you come to God expecting Him to meet you then you will find that He does not disappoint. Dan is expecting God to provide more of these encounters in the future so one can only imagine where this might lead.

You need to be open to God giving Him full access into your life trusting that He has your ultimate good in mind. That will help you to get yourself into a place where you can hear God Himself speak to you directly, or where you can hear Him speak to you through your circumstances, or hear Him speak to you through friends, family and even strangers. It may take you time to fully tune in to God but God is patient with you and will reward your efforts to reach out to Him, taking you on a journey unlike any that you could ever expect or imagine.

23. *How this author came to know God*

Growing up I was always curious to answer the question "Does God exist or not?", but there was far too much going on in my life for me to really sit down and try to answer it. From my perspective, I considered it to be a complex question and I did not know any one that really believed 100% beyond a shadow of a doubt that God existed.

So I put off answering the question. Even so there would be times when I would run across a pastor or church leader and would listen closely to what they said figuring that if anyone would know God they would. But they were too vague for me and still didn't answer all of my questions. I thought that no one could be 100% certain that God existed.

By age 32 I decided that I needed to examine the question more seriously. Does God exist or not? I wanted to know the answer, even if only for myself. Not trusting anyone else, I decided to read and study anything that I could find on the subject. I wanted an honest answer, and didn't want to be swayed by the opinion of any one person.

I have a mathematical, analytical type of mind so it was easy for me to see that this question requires a simple answer – either a YES God exists, or a NO He does not. There could be no in-between. I needed to know the answer and I was determined to find it.

But before I begin telling you about my search, let me digress. Let me go back to my childhood; that will give you a glimpse of who I am and will assist me in setting the stage for what was to come later.

I was born and raised in South Africa. The South Africa that I grew up in the 1960s 70s and 80s was the country of *apartheid* (racial segregation). White people, while only comprising 14 percent of the population, dominated the country politically and economically, owning most of the businesses and having the higher paying jobs. Black people had the menial jobs and, most significantly, did not have the vote: only white people could vote.

Black townships were separate from the white residential areas. In these townships black people lived in extreme poverty. A black person could work in a white area but if they were found in a white area at night without permission from their employer it usually meant certain imprisonment.

I was fortunate to be spared most hardship since I was born white. As a white South African I got an excellent school education at a whites-only school with facilities far superior to those at a black school. After completing school my grades were good enough to get me a corporate scholarship to a top university.

The South African apartheid system was enforced by a white dominated army and police force that maintained white domination at any cost. The state controlled the newspapers and also provided the schools with textbooks that were full of propaganda supporting the segregation of races.

I had begun to seriously question the apartheid system even while I was in primary school. In high school I became even more suspicious of those in power.

Why were our history textbooks distorting the truth? Why were the protectors of the people - the police - suppressing the black majority? Why were the black majority being denied the vote? Who could I trust to tell me the truth?

I tell you this to show you that I have always questioned things, and I certainly didn't trust anyone to tell me whether or not God existed.

South Africa had the draft and I was drafted into the army. The draft consisted of an initial two years in the military followed by one to three months a year for the next ten years in the military. There really was no choice as to whether you went into the military or not. The alternative was to go to prison for six years and that was not too appealing to me. I was forced against my will to support a system that I was convinced was immoral and was set to fail. This played a significant role in my decision to go and live in the USA in 1990 when the opportunity opened up to me.

I give you this information to let you know that I was born into a culture filled with lies and half truths. As a child I initially accepted things the way they were but as I grew older I began to question things and began searching out truth often putting aside preconceived notions that I had grown up with.

Coming back to the Christian theme of this book, my father, who did not attend church, took it upon him to send me to children's "Sunday School" two to three times a month. By the time I was thirteen I realized that my school friends that were going to my church had lives that were no different to the lives of those that did not go to church. I decided that church wasn't making any difference, so went home after children's church one day and told my father that I had decided that I didn't want to go to church anymore. He asked me why and after listening to my reasons he simply responded "Ok" and something along the lines of him having given me the opportunity to decide for myself - and that was that. I didn't go to church for a long time after that.

So I grew up never going to church as a teenager. I left school and went to university to study business & computers obtaining a Bachelors degree. I also met Lisa who would later become my wife while I was there. Lisa's mother went to an Episcopal church. On rare occasions I would out of a sense of duty accompany her mother and family to church. In church I would sit on the pew, look around and say to myself: "I don't get it? What is with these people? Where is their God? How do they even know that He exists, where is the proof? When it came time to receive communion I didn't take it because I didn't really believe in what it stood for and I couldn't take it in good conscience.

God and email.

After university I was drafted. When my two years of military draft were over I began working in the computer department of one of the largest electrical utilities in the world. Lisa and I got married and shortly thereafter I accepted a job offer in the USA. My motivation for leaving South Africa was to avoid end years of military draft, make more money and have a better environment in which to raise children. We lived in two states before moving to a small town outside Philadelphia.

For a number of years before this I had really begun to ask myself the question: Does God exist or not? I needed to know the truth. Little did I realize that God had placed that desire in me and was slowly drawing me to Himself.

I was living next-door to a young married couple Pam & William and their young sons Dylan and Brendan. We had a few barbeques and celebrated birthdays together and although we didn't really speak about God much I knew that he was a Christian. He was working with Scripture Union and was very active in his church; I even went to hear him speak once. The earth did not move for me and I still didn't "see" God in the church. After 11 months I was transferred to Atlanta GA.

A few days before I left Philadelphia for Atlanta I spoke to William about God but nothing in a conversation could probably ever have really convinced me of God's existence. I would probably have to study the case for the existence of God for myself.

The day before I left, William gave me a "One Year New Testament" - the New Testament of the Bible rearranged into 365 easy to manage daily readings. I resolved to myself to read it faithfully during the course of the next year. If I wanted to study the case for the existence of God in more depth than I had in the past, then this would be a good place to start.

While I had resolved to read the Bible, I also knew that I had to study more than just the Bible: I couldn't study just the Christian side of the story. It made sense that I also needed to study what people of other faiths had to say about the existence of God. What if the Muslims have the correct religion? What if the Jews have the correct religion? What about Hinduism, Buddhism, Confucianism? Perhaps there is no God and the atheists are right? What about what the scientific community has to say around things such as dinosaurs, fossils, big bang theory, evolution, carbon dating? I had a lot of questions.

I had grown up in a country that was considered to be a Christian country - much the same as America considers itself to be a Christian country. I knew that whatever I knew about God may have come from the environment that I grew up in. I resolved to try to put aside any preconceptions that I had as to whether God existed or not. I resolved to examine everything. There was to be no stone left unturned. Every question that I had was going to be answered so that I could make a decision that I could be at peace with. One thing was certain: I was never going to have to answer a question in this area ever again. I was going to be thorough. I wanted to find out the truth.

My mind is very mathematical - I like to resolve mathematical problems. I work with computers where I can prove things. Things are either correct and they work, or they are incorrect and do not work at all. All data in a computer can be broken down until it is either a one or a zero. There is no grey area of uncertainty in-between. Similarly, I reasoned that God either exists or He does not. There could be no in-between. I resolved that I was going to study what I could to find out for myself, in an unbiased fashion, whether or not God exists.

I continued reading the Bible daily for three weeks until unexpectedly receiving an email from William who had given me the "One Year New Testament". Not a big deal you might think but email was in its infancy then and few people used it. In addition William had no way of ever being able to afford a computer and to top it off he had been given this computer. In his email he even explained how he had been given the computer but I didn't think much of it at the time as I worked with computers daily.

God and email.

God was beginning to do something. Even though William and I now lived 800 miles apart I can look back now and see that God wanted to answer my questions about the Bible. He was putting William and I in touch. At the time though, I would never even have considered this as being a remote possibility. My experience in later years would also come to confirm that whenever I read the Bible seriously looking for answers then answers would come my way, and these answers would often come from unexpected places. I had certainly not experienced this with any of the other books from any of the other religions. I can see now that God was starting to answer my questions yet at the time I certainly didn't recognize this.

I began to pose some detailed questions to William about passages in the Bible that I didn't understand. So detailed in fact that William sometimes took days to reflect on them and compose a reply. He never once complained about the number of questions but steadily answered them one by one. This process of us emailing each other continued on a regular basis for nine months.

At the same time that I was doing this I examined the Islamic faith. I discovered that Muslims essentially believe in the story of the Bible up to the time of Abraham. They believe that Mohammed is a prophet of God. They even believe that Jesus is a prophet yet they do not study the claims made about Jesus – that he claimed to be God and that he rose from the dead – because they believe that the Biblical texts have been corrupted over the years. I needed to examine whether this was really the case. A more detailed examination of the life of Mohammed also revealed a man organizing wars against other people, a man supportive of domestic violence and a man given to fits of rage. I could see some good in the Islamic devotedness to God and the frequency of their prayers but the character traits of the man Mohammed cast a shadow over Islam for me.

I looked at Buddhism and found that it has its roots in Hinduism, so I turned towards studying what the Hindus believe.

The Hindus puzzled me the most. Thousands of gods are worshipped making the religion seem very complex to me. It made sense therefore to try and find the most powerful of these gods but I was never able to single out this "god". I searched sacred Hindu texts but reached a dead end there as well. I honed in on the Hindu belief in reincarnation. The goal of life as reincarnation as taught is to be "a good person" in life, so that one can be reincarnated as a better person in ones next life and to have this cycle repeat until one finally reaches an everlasting state of Nirvana (supposedly achieved by the Yogis), in which one is free of Karmic actions and is not bound by the cycle of reincarnation. The more I examined this, the more it bothered me. I did not know how anyone could achieve this state of perfection by being a "good person" all of the time. I know that even though I tried to live what I considered to be a "good life" as a "good person", I could never hope to be perfect all of the time.

Since the first books of the Christian Bible have their roots in the Jewish Torah, I resolved that I needed to examine the Jewish faith as well. I was astonished to find out how similar the Old Testament and the Torah are. More importantly, I found fascinating passages in the writings of the Old Testament such as Isaiah 53, which predicted the coming of Jesus.

While all of the religions may have some degree of the truth I decided that I needed to focus on the aspects of each religion that appeared to have the most truth in them.

As I could make out, the Muslims, Jews, and Christians of the world believed in the same God up to the time of Abraham. It was after Abraham's time that the various faiths seemed to drastically diverge. Also as far as I could see, if the majority of the world's population believed in this one God, the God of Abraham, then there might be more to this God than that which first meets the eye. I resolved to study this God further. That was a significant step forward in my understanding of God.

Since people were bringing the validity of the Bible and its historical accuracy into question, I needed to answer for myself whether the Bible is just a book of stories or whether is it is in fact true and accurate. The research that I did pointed to the fact that the Bible is based on documents that have been remarkably preserved throughout the ages and accurately reflect the original documents. It appeared that holy men of God acting under the fear of God and trying to please God, throughout the centuries would have ensured that the text was faithfully recorded down through the centuries. This argument is further validated by the discovery of the Dead Sea Scrolls which happened in 1947. The Dead Sea Scrolls were written before AD100, yet they include a copy of the book of Isaiah that, when compared to the modern Bible, is to all extents and purposes an exact copy. That alone gives greater credibility to the rest of the Bible and provides a good case for the fact that the original texts have not been altered over the centuries.

I also honed in on the Biblical stories in the Bible looking for scientific evidence that would contradict them. I had to wrestle with issues outside the Bible such as dinosaurs, carbon dating, the Big Bang theory and the like to determine if the Bible was contradicting them. I looked at the reliability of carbon dating. I looked at the statistically small chance of this planet occurring by chance out of nothing.

While there were still questions open, there was no direct scientific proof against the Biblical record.

I looked at the mind boggling stories of miracles in the Bible trying to understand them; but I had to concede that if God existed and wanted to perform a miracle then by virtue of the fact that He is God He could do anything he wanted to. How could I exclude the possibility of miracles if God existed?

Eventually after nine months and many e-mails to William I got to the point where I had examined all of the evidence at my disposal and had to make a decision. Does God exist or not? As far as I was concerned, the vast majority of the available evidence rested on the side of God. I was 96 percent convinced that God existed. That was a pretty high percentage in my mind. At that point, based on the evidence that I had examined, I decided that I could make a decision that God most likely existed. I believed that I had found the truth.

It stands to reason that if God exists, then I can pray to him. Still I needed to be honest to myself about the element of doubt that I had. So I prayed a prayer that was to change my life. The essence of what I prayed is contained in "the skeptic's prayer", a prayer that I found in the book *The Handbook of Christian Apologetics* by Peter Kreeft & Ronald K. Tacelli:

God, I don't know whether you even exist. I'm a skeptic. I doubt. I think you may be only a myth. But I'm not certain (at least not when I'm completely honest with myself). So if you do exist, and if you really did promise to reward all seekers, you must be hearing me now. So I hereby declare myself a seeker, a seeker of the truth, whatever it is and wherever it is. I want to know the truth and live the truth. If you are the truth please help me.

But following on from this prayer I was still probing deeper into the Christian faith. I had to be able to prove that Jesus is God's son and that He rose from the dead. That after all is the central claim of Christianity. If that were to be disproved then everything would all the claims of Christianity would collapse.

I couldn't understand why a God that cared for humanity would punish all mankind as a consequence of **one** man's actions. How could he punish me for something that Adam did? It didn't seem fair. But as much as I didn't understand that I did see in the Bible (Romans 5:10) that "Just as **one** man (Adam) caused our separation from God, **one** man (Jesus) caused our reconciliation to God". If one man could separate us from God and one man could reconcile us to God then, as much as I didn't understand it, it at least seemed fair on the part of God.

There are many arguments that I could now give you to support the fact that Jesus is God's son but, for me at the time, the most compelling evidence was an argument based on the author CS Lewis' writings. CS Lewis was a professor of Medieval and Renaissance Literature at the University of Cambridge. His argument (in slightly modified form) is presented below:

Most people will say that Jesus walked this earth and that he was a good man and a great moral teacher. If you can agree with me on that, I now have to ask you a question:

Can a good man tell a lie?

A good man and a great moral teacher cannot tell a lie for it would discredit him. This good man and great moral teacher said: "Let not your heart be troubled: you believe in God, believe also in me" (John 14:1). He also said "I and the Father (God) are one" and "...No man comes to the Father (God) but by me" (John 14:6).

If Jesus was a good man and a great moral teacher then He could not be a liar, so:

Jesus must be the Son of God.

I knew that I had come to the end of my search. I knew that I had found the truth. I knew from my earlier studies that the Biblical record is accurate and that I could trust the writings in the Bible, it stood to reason therefore that the claims of Jesus as expressed in the Bible must be true. He could not be a liar and yet he claimed to be none other than the son of God. This had to be true. I had come to a decision: Jesus must be the son of God. The Biblical record has Jesus rising from the dead. If I am to trust the Biblical record then this has to be true as well.

Strangely enough, this decision gave me a deep sense of satisfaction. Little did I ever suspect that this decision was about to change my entire life. Up until now I had knowledge *about God* but I didn't *know God.* I was about to get to know God – to really get to know God.

I thought that I had everything about God all figured out and didn't expect anything to change in my life. I thought that I should probably go to church occasionally and read the Bible but I didn't expect anything more. My faith in God was still private and internal. I didn't know anyone that knew God. I had been conditioned by my previous experiences with people that went to church. None of these people even though they went to church really knew God. So in short I expected my life now that I was a Christian to be basically the same as it was before. This was not to be.

I began to pray – albeit silently- just a brief two minute prayer each day. It was not a religious prayer, just a sincere honest prayer to God while lying flat on my back in bed before I went to sleep. Nothing overly spiritual about that but it was sincere. Added to this I began to read the Bible more; primarily because I now wanted to understand it better. I still had this impression of God sitting in the sky somewhere watching us rushing about down below on the earth. I was about to find out that I did not understand the Christian life fully - that God wanted to become actively involved in my life. My life began to change.

You see the Holy Spirit had taken over and was going to change my life as only He can. Up to now I had not even been aware of the Holy Spirit. The Christian churches talk about Father, Son and Holy Spirit - the doctrine of the trinity - where all three are one but I had not even given the Holy Spirit the slightest thought.

My prayer had declared me to be a seeker of truth. The Holy Spirit is the Spirit of Truth. Without consciously knowing it, I had found the truth that I was seeking for. Over time I began to understand that:

- I struggled with the concept of being "born again" because I did not understand it. Yet in John 3:7 Jesus said: Do not marvel that I said that you must be born again.

- Eventually I discovered that Jesus was talking about my spirit. That my spirit could be born again.

- Jesus said in John 3:5 Unless one is born of water and the spirit, He cannot enter the kingdom of God.

- I discovered that Jesus sent me this Holy Spirit or Spirit of Truth:
  John 14:16&17, And I (Jesus) will pray to the Father and He will give you another Helper, that He may abide will you forever - the Spirit of Truth.

- And I discovered that this Spirit lives in me:
  1 Cor 3:16, Know ye not that ye are the temple of God, and the Spirit of God dwelleth in you.

So I have this Holy Spirit living in me. Looking back it all seems clearer and easier to explain. At the time however when it was all beginning to come together there were times when I was tempted to give up and go back to my old beliefs - they certainly involved less mental effort. What kept me going through all of these mental struggles was the knowledge that I had made a decision based on all of the facts at my disposal. I could not back out – I had, after all, examined all the facts. There is no other alternative.

I was convinced then that I had found Truth and to this day I am even more convinced that I have. It is events such as these in the next chapter that have added to my conviction that I have found the Truth.

24. Growing in Christ and the Holy Spirit

Learning from others who mirror the life of Christ

After I had become a Christian I moved to Dallas Texas where I decided that if I wanted to be a follower of Christ then it made sense that I should probably attend church occasionally. So I went to the first church down the road, found that the people there were friendly enough and I started attending church regularly. For the first time in my life I went to church because I really wanted to. I cannot recall really wanting to go to church before that. Sure, there were things that I didn't like or understand in that church but I was prepared to look beyond that and embrace that which I did understand.

At church I met, for the first time, someone who modeled the Christian life as I would expect it to be lived. She taught Sunday school, had a good Christian family, and also had something else I could not quite understand. In due course I would come to understand that it was the Holy Spirit who comes to live in all of us who are followers of Christ. I listened to her and began to learn from what she taught. I could not fault her teaching - it all came from the Bible. Most importantly she lived what she talked. I was encouraged by her example and began to learn from what she taught.

When God really started to get involved.

About this time my wife Lisa decided that she wanted to go to and visit a church in Pensacola Florida where they were experiencing what they called a religious revival. Thousands of people were lining up outside the church on a daily basis from early morning just to get inside when the doors finally opened in the evening. I tried to remain unimpressed. I reasoned that if God was prepared to show up in church there, He could certainly show up in my church as well.

As soon as I resolved that God could show up in my church if He wanted to, I got a phone call from someone who I had never met before asking me if I could do a week's work for him in Florida. Working in Dallas and Atlanta were the closest that I had ever come to working in Florida before. Nevertheless, the work that he wanted me to do matched my computer skills exactly, so we set a date for the work to be done.

When the date for my assignment approached I called him and asked him for directions from the airport to the office. I didn't even know which city he was in. It turned out that the job was in Pensacola Florida the same city that the church with the revival was in. My heart raced. I was not in the habit of traveling on business at that point in my life. This was more than coincidence. I ended up making plane reservations for my family to go with me. I would work while they enjoyed the vacation. At night we would investigate this church. We stayed on the beachfront. The rental car turned out unexpectedly to be a convertible. Things were working out very well.

After my first day at work we went to the church and there my heart sank: there was a long, long line of people waiting to get in to the church. They had even parked their own deckchairs outside the church to wait out the day and get a front row seat inside when the doors finally opened. Arriving at the end of the day I would not make it into the main building, and would have to watch the service on a movie screen in one of the side rooms. I was not impressed.

Immediately after the service things began to improve. I met someone who was homeless who told me that he stood in line from early morning every day, was always first in line and offered to keep me a place in line each day so that when I arrived from work at the end of the day I would not be at the back of the line. After doing this for one day my wife decided to join the line while I was at work and I would join her later.

For an entire week I was first into church every day despite the thousands of people lining up all day to get in. A bonus was that because I went on business, my company picked up almost the entire bill for the whole trip.

It was a blessing from God. God was starting to show me that He would move mountains and open doors for me if I kept my heart pure and remained open to His working in my life.

Executive Ministries, Greenville North Carolina

I had heard about a branch of Campus Crusade for Christ called Executive Ministries based in Greenville, South Carolina. Since I am also in business, I was interested in what they were doing and I applied to join them. They turned me down because I did not as of then have a Green Card to work in the USA.

But God saw my interest and soon after that my boss called me and told me that he had a client that he needed me to visit in none other than ... Greenville, South Carolina. Even though my boss was not a Christian he used the curious phrase that, due to my skills matching the client's requirements 100 percent, this assignment was a "match made in heaven".

There were two flight segments to my first trip into Greenville and both of them got my attention. On the first leg from Dallas to Atlanta I sat next to a man reading the Bible. On the second leg from Atlanta to Greenville I sat next to a lady reading some Christian literature. I started talking to her and discovered that she was from ... Executive Ministries! This was the exact organization that I had expressed interest in joining!

She gave me all of the information related to the Executive Ministries meetings that were held in Greenville, South Carolina. Needless to say, for the rest of the year that I worked in Greenville I attended a weekly Wednesday morning meeting of Executive Ministries.

God was amazingly showing me that He is directly interested in all the details of my life, without me even asking Him to get involved. I had not prayed for any of this to happen. It had all just unfolded around me. It gave me a huge boost to my faith.

So now that God has shown that He is directly interested in the details of my life, the life of faith becomes so much easier to live. I see God in all that is happening in my life.

We see confirmation of what was happening in my life in John 14:21 where Jesus says that "He that hath my commandments and keepeth them, he it is that loveth me; and he that loveth me shall be loved of my Father, and I will love him and will manifest myself to him."

But God moved from doing things in my life and showing me things about Himself to directly "speaking" to me. It was just a small quiet internal voice at first, a kind of "knowing". I began to pay attention to it more and more. It is an integral part of the relationship that God wants with me just as it is part of the relationship that God wants with you.

How I heard God speak about a sick co-worker.

Hugh and I had briefly worked together in San Francisco on a four month project. He liked my work and asked me to fly in from Dallas, where I was living at the time, to do some more work for him in London for a week or two. I eagerly accepted, who wouldn't want a trip to London, England?

In the office in London I was quietly sitting next to a Hugh, minding my own business, when that small internal voice from God impressed upon my mind that Hugh was sick.

So I started reasoning with God in my mind: "So what if he is sick?"
But then I asked the question that was to set in motion a whole chain of events, "God if you are telling me that Hugh is sick then why did you tell me and what should I do about it?"
God responded instantly, "Tell him".
"I can't do that", I replied.

God and email.

"Yes you can", replied God.
"I can't do that", I replied.
"Yes you can", replied God.
So in the end I gave in and called Hugh aside into a deserted hallway to ask him if he was sick. I had no idea what the response would be and didn't want anyone else around to hear what I had to say.

"Are you sick?" I asked Hugh.
"No" he calmly replied.
"Are you sure?" I responded.
By this time my heart had sunk and I was trying to redeem the situation.
"Do you have a cold?" I asked him.
"No" he replied quizzically.
"Are you sure?" I responded.
"Yes, why?" he replied.
I then proceeded to tell him outright that God had told me that he was sick. He gave me this "you must be crazy" look and told me that he didn't believe in God.

I asked him if he would go with me to the cafeteria and there we had an open talk about Christianity for about 30 minutes. He left stating that he still didn't believe in God. I flew home thinking that I had now gone crazy for sure, was hearing voices, and I certainly couldn't expect any more work from that company.

Unsurprisingly I heard nothing more from Hugh for the next nine months. Suddenly and unexpectedly I got a phone call from a secretary of his in California. Hugh was dead – he had died suddenly from pancreatic cancer. They had found my name and phone number in his diary and were calling me to let me know just in case I was close to him.

I hope that as his last days approached Hugh remembered what I had told him in London and that he had come to believe in Jesus and to gain eternal life through that. But as much as I hope that, I must confess that I just don't know what happened in the final days of Hugh's life. What I do know now is that this is no game - the consequences are eternal.

How I heard God speak about "Gillian".

On the trip back from London I sat next to a young lady in her early twenties. She was from Sacramento, California and we began to exchange a few words. I asked her what she was doing in London and she explained that she was a student. She had spent three months there and was going home to visit her family.

I also discovered that she had had a roommate in London that had got on her nerves more and more while she was living there. She was leaving London and she was glad to see the end of her. She asked me whether I was married, whether I had children, where I lived. There was polite conversation for a while, until after a while, we lapsed into silence for the ten hour flight ahead.

About three hours into the flight I was sitting quietly, reading my Bible, when God impressed the name Gillian on my mind and I felt that He wanted me to ask her about Gillian.

"I can't do that", I thought.
"Ask her", said the Lord more firmly this time (you see God is patient).
"I can't do that - she will think that I'm crazy", I responded.
"Ask her", said the Lord more firmly this time.
I gritted my teeth and turned to her: "Tell me about Gillian", I said.
She replied, "Which Gillian?"
She probed further, "Gillian in London or Gillian in Florida?"
"I don't know - you tell me", I responded.

She then proceeded to tell me that her friend Gillian in Florida came to live with her in London and was her roommate for three months. God had given me the name of her roommate that had got on her nerves!

Then she caught herself: "Tell me how you knew about Gillian?"

For the rest of the flight I had a captive audience as I shared with her the power of the Holy Spirit and what it means to know this Jesus Christ.

Selling all to follow God.

I got to a point in my life where I quit my job in the USA, sold my house and two cars, and took my wife and two young children to Scotland in response to a call from God.

The call came in stages. First I had a dream about a place in Europe. Then an angel from Scotland visited me in a dream that was unlike any other dream that I have ever had.

Immediately after that I came across a Christian organization called YWAM (Youth With A Mission) and discovered that it was looking for a computer manager. I thought that this organization sounded like the type of Christian organization that I would want to join so I investigated further and found out that the position was in Scotland. This was getting interesting.

The curious turn of events settled this in my mind as being something from God so off my family and I went to live in Scotland. Fortunately for me I am blessed with a wonderful wife who willingly went along with the whole idea. God had obviously spoken to her about this as well. I am blessed to be married to this amazing woman.

When we got to Scotland I discovered that the YWAM facility was the place in Europe that I had dreamed about months before.

While living in Scotland for a year we had no income since we were only volunteering. Our entry visa granted by the government did not permit us to work. Despite this we managed to rent a house and get by for an entire year. For someone such as me, who was used to earning an excellent salary, this alone was remarkable.

In an effort to keep this brief I will just say that we met some incredible faith filled Christians there, and had a wonderful year, the stories of which could easily fill another book.

25.   Final thoughts

I enjoy my real and active relationship with God. I have come to rely on him more and more. The more I look to him, the more he helps me and the more powerful the results. The results come because I lean on Him and talk about Jesus. Jesus is the key. The Holy Spirit is the Spirit of Truth and witnesses of Jesus:

John 16:13&14 "When the **Spirit of Truth** has come, He will guide you into all truth; for He will not speak on his own authority, but whatever He hears He will speak; and He will tell you of things to come. He will glorify Me (Jesus) for He will take of what is mine (Jesus') and declare it to you."

If I look back on what was important I notice that:

- I examined the evidence for myself - I never stopped searching, and the more I sought to resolve the questions I had, the more answers I found.
- I didn't place any limitations on God and I didn't have preconceived notions of who He is.
- I was also prepared to accept as probable any argument that I could not logically disprove letting the weight of that evidence accumulate.
- In the end I needed to embrace Jesus. My prayer to receive Jesus was critically important. Without embracing Jesus and personally receiving him nothing would have happened.
- I began to pray. Initially I prayed only a mere two minutes a day but that was enough for God who began to answer those prayers.
- After this I came to understand the "Holy Spirit", the spirit of God that resides in us and awakens us to the things of God.

Now things have progressed beyond that and I have what I would call a "relationship" with God. As an indirect result, my time spent in daily prayer and Bible reading has increased in my life. Spending time with God has become something that I want to do. It is exciting for me to know that a loving God wants to talk to us!

I had started off not trusting anyone and was looking for a truthful answer to my question "Does God exist?" Little did I know that God's *Holy Spirit* is the *Spirit of Truth* and that in my search for truth the Holy Spirit would direct me to the inevitable conclusion that God exists. I ended up finding an answer - God does exist but not in the way that I ever expected. I did not know that this God would seek to call me friend and would want to establish a vibrant living relationship with me.

Friend, this Jesus Christ wants to establish the same vibrant living relationship with you today! Will you let Him do that? Why don't you ask him begin to establish a relationship with you now? You can pray to him anywhere; why not do it now?

26. Contact the author

Perhaps you have a story of how God spoke to you or perhaps you have a story about something miraculous that He did in your life, if so I would love to hear about it.

I can be reached via email at:

MarkCraythorn@hotmail.com

27.   *Acknowledgements*

To Lisa, my wife, who has gone on this adventure of knowing Christ with me; you have taught me so much and are an inspiration to me.

To my children Michael & Melissa who mean the world to me and who I have dragged around the world on my travels; thank you for putting up with me.

To all of those who graciously agreed to let me put their stories in this book; my faith in God has grown by leaps and bounds because of you. A few of your names have been changed but most have not. You know who you are. Thank you so, so much!

28. *Appendix: The Bible - Book of Mark*

I find it amazing that God chooses to use a book such as the Bible that was compiled so many years ago, to speak into our lives today. If you question God's existence or if you have questions that you would like to ask Him, you will find that if you seriously study this Bible, God will over time bring answers to you. One of the keys to studying is persistence. I am not talking about a superficial reading of the text; I am talking about reading with an open mind and seriously looking for answers.

The sheer size of the Bible can make it rather daunting. Confusing the issue is the vast array of Bibles available today The English in some versions can be old fashioned so I recommend that you find a Bible that is published in a format that you find easy to read; doing that will make it much so easier to begin reading. Once you have selected a Bible simply find a good place in it to start reading. My recommendation is to start with the Book of Mark.

Versions of Bibles that I have personally found to be useful are:

* *NIV (New International Version) Study Bible* published by Zondervan
* *The Message* by Eugene Peterson

These are however not the only versions that I recommend: there are many more that have helped me over the years. I merely found these texts to be a good starting place for me personally.

I have included the **Book of Mark** from the King James version of the Bible for easy reference below. The English is not modern but it contains the same message as all other Bible versions:

1:1 The beginning of the gospel of Jesus Christ, the Son of God

1:2 As it is written in the prophets, Behold, I send my messenger before thy face, which shall prepare thy way before thee.

1:3 The voice of one crying in the wilderness, Prepare ye the way of the Lord, make his paths straight.

1:4 John did baptize in the wilderness, and preach the baptism of repentance for the remission of sins.

1:5 And there went out unto him all the land of Judaea, and they of Jerusalem, and were all baptized of him in the river of Jordan, confessing their sins.

1:6 And John was clothed with camel's hair, and with a girdle of a skin about his loins; and he did eat locusts and wild honey

1:7 And preached, saying, There cometh one mightier than I after me, the latchet of whose shoes I am not worthy to stoop down and unloose.

1:8 I indeed have baptized you with water: but he shall baptize you with the Holy Ghost.

1:9 And it came to pass in those days, that Jesus came from Nazareth of Galilee, and was baptized of John in Jordan.

1:10 And straightway coming up out of the water, he saw the heavens opened, and the Spirit like a dove descending upon him

1:11 And there came a voice from heaven, saying, Thou art my beloved Son, in whom I am well pleased.

1:12 And immediately the spirit driveth him into the wilderness.

1:13 And he was there in the wilderness forty days, tempted of Satan; and was with the wild beasts; and the angels ministered unto him.

1:14 Now after that John was put in prison, Jesus came into Galilee, preaching the gospel of the kingdom of God

1:15 And saying, The time is fulfilled, and the kingdom of God is at hand: repent ye, and believe the gospel.

1:16 Now as he walked by the sea of Galilee, he saw Simon and Andrew his brother casting a net into the sea: for they were fishers.

1:17 And Jesus said unto them, Come ye after me, and I will make you to become fishers of men.

1:18 And straightway they forsook their nets, and followed him.

1:19 And when he had gone a little farther thence, he saw James the son of Zebedee, and John his brother, who also were in the ship mending their nets.

1:20 And straightway he called them: and they left their father Zebedee in the ship with the hired servants, and went after him.

1:21 And they went into Capernaum; and straightway on the sabbath day he entered into the synagogue, and taught.

1:22 And they were astonished at his doctrine: for he taught them as one that had authority, and not as the scribes.

1:23 And there was in their synagogue a man with an unclean spirit; and he cried out,

1:24 Saying, Let us alone; what have we to do with thee, thou Jesus of Nazareth? art thou come to destroy us? I know thee who thou art, the Holy One of God.

1:25 And Jesus rebuked him, saying, Hold thy peace, and come out of him.

1:26 And when the unclean spirit had torn him, and cried with a loud voice, he came out of him.

1:27 And they were all amazed, insomuch that they questioned among themselves, saying, What thing is this? what new doctrine is this? for with authority commandeth he even the unclean spirits, and they do obey him.

1:28 And immediately his fame spread abroad throughout all the region round about Galilee.

1:29 And forthwith, when they were come out of the synagogue, they entered into the house of Simon and Andrew, with James and John.

1:30 But Simon's wife's mother lay sick of a fever, and anon they tell him of her.

1:31 And he came and took her by the hand, and lifted her up; and immediately the fever left her, and she ministered unto them.

1:32 And at even, when the sun did set, they brought unto him all that were diseased, and them that were possessed with devils.

1:33 And all the city was gathered together at the door.

1:34 And he healed many that were sick of divers diseases, and cast out many devils; and suffered not the devils to speak, because they knew him.

1:35 And in the morning, rising up a great while before day, he went out, and departed into a solitary place, and there prayed.

1:36 And Simon and they that were with him followed after him.

1:37 And when they had found him, they said unto him, All men seek for thee.

1:38 And he said unto them, Let us go into the next towns, that I may preach there also: for therefore came I forth.

1:39 And he preached in their synagogues throughout all Galilee, and cast out devils.

1:40 And there came a leper to him, beseeching him, and kneeling down to him, and saying unto him, If thou wilt, thou canst make me clean.

1:41 And Jesus, moved with compassion, put forth his hand, and touched him, and saith unto him, I will; be thou clean.

1:42 And as soon as he had spoken, immediately the leprosy departed from him, and he was cleansed.

1:43 And he straitly charged him, and forthwith sent him away;

1:44 And saith unto him, See thou say nothing to any man: but go thy way, shew thyself to the priest, and offer for thy cleansing those things which Moses commanded, for a testimony unto them.

1:45 But he went out, and began to publish it much, and to blaze abroad the matter, insomuch that Jesus could no more openly enter into the city, but was without in desert places: and they came to him from every quarter.

2:1 And again he entered into Capernaum after some days; and it was noised that he was in the house.

2:2 And straightway many were gathered together, insomuch that there was no room to receive them, no, not so much as about the door: and he preached the word unto them.

2:3 And they come unto him, bringing one sick of the palsy, which was borne of four.

2:4 And when they could not come nigh unto him for the press, they uncovered the roof where he was: and when they had broken it up, they let down the bed wherein the sick of the palsy lay.

2:5 When Jesus saw their faith, he said unto the sick of the palsy, Son, thy sins be forgiven thee.

2:6 But there was certain of the scribes sitting there, and reasoning in their hearts,

2:7 Why doth this man thus speak blasphemies? who can forgive sins but God only?

2:8 And immediately when Jesus perceived in his spirit that they so reasoned within themselves, he said unto them, Why reason ye these things in your hearts?

2:9 Whether is it easier to say to the sick of the palsy, Thy sins be forgiven thee; or to say, Arise, and take up thy bed, and walk?

2:10 But that ye may know that the Son of man hath power on earth to forgive sins, (he saith to the sick of the palsy,)

2:11 I say unto thee, Arise, and take up thy bed, and go thy way into thine house.

2:12 And immediately he arose, took up the bed, and went forth before them all; insomuch that they were all amazed, and glorified God, saying, We never saw it on this fashion.

2:13 And he went forth again by the sea side; and all the multitude resorted unto him, and he taught them.

2:14 And as he passed by, he saw Levi the son of Alphaeus sitting at the receipt of custom, and said unto him, Follow me. And he arose and followed him.

2:15 And it came to pass, that, as Jesus sat at meat in his house, many publicans and sinners sat also together with Jesus and his disciples: for there were many, and they followed him.

2:16 And when the scribes and Pharisees saw him eat with publicans and sinners, they said unto his disciples, How is it that he eateth and drinketh with publicans and sinners?

2:17 When Jesus heard it, he saith unto them, They that are whole have no need of the physician, but they that are sick: I came not to call the righteous, but sinners to repentance.

2:18 And the disciples of John and of the Pharisees used to fast: and they come and say unto him, Why do the disciples of John and of the Pharisees fast, but thy disciples fast not?

2:19 And Jesus said unto them, Can the children of the bridechamber fast, while the bridegroom is with them? as long as they have the bridegroom with them, they cannot fast.

2:20 But the days will come, when the bridegroom shall be taken away from them, and then shall they fast in those days.

2:21 No man also seweth a piece of new cloth on an old garment: else the new piece that filled it up taketh away from the old, and the rent is made worse.

2:22 And no man putteth new wine into old bottles: else the new wine doth burst the bottles, and the wine is spilled, and the bottles will be marred: but new wine must be put into new bottles.

2:23 And it came to pass, that he went through the corn fields on the sabbath day; and his disciples began, as they went, to pluck the ears of corn.

2:24 And the Pharisees said unto him, Behold, why do they on the sabbath day that which is not lawful?

2:25 And he said unto them, Have ye never read what David did, when he had need, and was an hungred, he, and they that were with him?

2:26 How he went into the house of God in the days of Abiathar the high priest, and did eat the shewbread, which is not lawful to eat but for the priests, and gave also to them which were with him?

2:27 And he said unto them, The sabbath was made for man, and not man for the sabbath:

2:28 Therefore the Son of man is Lord also of the sabbath.

3:1 And he entered again into the synagogue; and there was a man there which had a withered hand.

3:2 And they watched him, whether he would heal him on the sabbath day; that they might accuse him.

3:3 And he saith unto the man which had the withered hand, Stand forth.

3:4 And he saith unto them, Is it lawful to do good on the sabbath days, or to do evil? to save life, or to kill? But they held their peace.

3:5 And when he had looked round about on them with anger, being grieved for the hardness of their hearts, he saith unto the man,

Stretch forth thine hand. And he stretched it out: and his hand was restored whole as the other.

3:6 And the Pharisees went forth, and straightway took counsel with the Herodians against him, how they might destroy him.

3:7 But Jesus withdrew himself with his disciples to the sea: and a great multitude from Galilee followed him, and from Judaea, **3:8** And from Jerusalem, and from Idumaea, and from beyond Jordan; and they about Tyre and Sidon, a great multitude, when they had heard what great things he did, came unto him.

3:9 And he spake to his disciples, that a small ship should wait on him because of the multitude, lest they should throng him.

3:10 For he had healed many; insomuch that they pressed upon him for to touch him, as many as had plagues.

3:11 And unclean spirits, when they saw him, fell down before him, and cried, saying, Thou art the Son of God.

3:12 And he straitly charged them that they should not make him known.

3:13 And he goeth up into a mountain, and calleth unto him whom he would: and they came unto him.

3:14 And he ordained twelve, that they should be with him, and that he might send them forth to preach,

3:15 And to have power to heal sicknesses, and to cast out devils: **3:16** And Simon he surnamed Peter;

3:17 And James the son of Zebedee, and John the brother of James; and he surnamed them Boanerges, which is, The sons of thunder: **3:18** And Andrew, and Philip, and Bartholomew, and Matthew, and Thomas, and James the son of Alphaeus, and Thaddaeus, and Simon the Canaanite,

3:19 And Judas Iscariot, which also betrayed him: and they went into an house.

3:20 And the multitude cometh together again, so that they could not so much as eat bread.

3:21 And when his friends heard of it, they went out to lay hold on him: for they said, He is beside himself.

3:22 And the scribes which came down from Jerusalem said, He hath Beelzebub, and by the prince of the devils casteth he out devils.

3:23 And he called them unto him, and said unto them in parables, How can Satan cast out Satan?

3:24 And if a kingdom be divided against itself, that kingdom cannot stand.

3:25 And if a house be divided against itself, that house cannot stand.

3:26 And if Satan rise up against himself, and be divided, he cannot stand, but hath an end.

3:27 No man can enter into a strong man's house, and spoil his goods, except he will first bind the strong man; and then he will spoil his house.

3:28 Verily I say unto you, All sins shall be forgiven unto the sons of men, and blasphemies wherewith soever they shall blaspheme:

3:29 But he that shall blaspheme against the Holy Ghost hath never forgiveness, but is in danger of eternal damnation.

3:30 Because they said, He hath an unclean spirit.

3:31 There came then his brethren and his mother, and, standing without, sent unto him, calling him.

3:32 And the multitude sat about him, and they said unto him, Behold, thy mother and thy brethren without seek for thee.

3:33 And he answered them, saying, Who is my mother, or my brethren?

3:34 And he looked round about on them which sat about him, and said, Behold my mother and my brethren! **3:35** For whosoever shall do the will of God, the same is my brother, and my sister, and mother.

4:1 And he began again to teach by the sea side: and there was gathered unto him a great multitude, so that he entered into a ship, and sat in the sea; and the whole multitude was by the sea on the land.

4:2 And he taught them many things by parables, and said unto them in his doctrine,

4:3 Hearken; Behold, there went out a sower to sow:

4:4 And it came to pass, as he sowed, some fell by the way side, and the fowls of the air came and devoured it up.

4:5 And some fell on stony ground, where it had not much earth;

and immediately it sprang up, because it had no depth of earth:

4:6 But when the sun was up, it was scorched; and because it had no root, it withered away.

4:7 And some fell among thorns, and the thorns grew up, and choked it, and it yielded no fruit.

4:8 And other fell on good ground, and did yield fruit that sprang up and increased; and brought forth, some thirty, and some sixty, and some an hundred.

4:9 And he said unto them, He that hath ears to hear, let him hear.

4:10 And when he was alone, they that were about him with the twelve asked of him the parable.

4:11 And he said unto them, Unto you it is given to know the mystery of the kingdom of God: but unto them that are without, all these things are done in parables:

4:12 That seeing they may see, and not perceive; and hearing they may hear, and not understand; lest at any time they should be converted, and their sins should be forgiven them.

4:13 And he said unto them, Know ye not this parable? and how then will ye know all parables?

4:14 The sower soweth the word.

4:15 And these are they by the way side, where the word is sown; but when they have heard, Satan cometh immediately, and taketh away the word that was sown in their hearts.

4:16 And these are they likewise which are sown on stony ground; who, when they have heard the word, immediately receive it with gladness;

4:17 And have no root in themselves, and so endure but for a time: afterward, when affliction or persecution ariseth for the word's sake, immediately they are offended.

4:18 And these are they which are sown among thorns; such as hear the word,

4:19 And the cares of this world, and the deceitfulness of riches, and the lusts of other things entering in, choke the word, and it becometh unfruitful.

4:20 And these are they which are sown on good ground; such as hear the word, and receive it, and bring forth fruit, some thirtyfold, some sixty, and some an hundred.

4:21 And he said unto them, Is a candle brought to be put under a bushel, or under a bed? and not to be set on a candlestick?

4:22 For there is nothing hid, which shall not be manifested; neither was any thing kept secret, but that it should come abroad.

4:23 If any man have ears to hear, let him hear.

4:24 And he said unto them, Take heed what ye hear: with what measure ye mete, it shall be measured to you: and unto you that hear shall more be given.

4:25 For he that hath, to him shall be given: and he that hath not, from him shall be taken even that which he hath.

4:26 And he said, So is the kingdom of God, as if a man should cast seed into the ground;

4:27 And should sleep, and rise night and day, and the seed should spring and grow up, he knoweth not how.

4:28 For the earth bringeth forth fruit of herself; first the blade, then the ear, after that the full corn in the ear.

4:29 But when the fruit is brought forth, immediately he putteth in the sickle, because the harvest is come.

4:30 And he said, Whereunto shall we liken the kingdom of God? or with what comparison shall we compare it?

4:31 It is like a grain of mustard seed, which, when it is sown in the earth, is less than all the seeds that be in the earth:

4:32 But when it is sown, it groweth up, and becometh greater than all herbs, and shooteth out great branches; so that the fowls of the air may lodge under the shadow of it.

4:33 And with many such parables spake he the word unto them, as they were able to hear it.

4:34 But without a parable spake he not unto them: and when they were alone, he expounded all things to his disciples.

4:35 And the same day, when the even was come, he saith unto them, Let us pass over unto the other side.

4:36 And when they had sent away the multitude, they took him even as he was in the ship. And there were also with him other little ships.

4:37 And there arose a great storm of wind, and the waves beat into the ship, so that it was now full.

4:38 And he was in the hinder part of the ship, asleep on a pillow: and they awake him, and say unto him, Master, carest thou not that we perish?

4:39 And he arose, and rebuked the wind, and said unto the sea, Peace, be still. And the wind ceased, and there was a great calm.

4:40 And he said unto them, Why are ye so fearful? how is it that ye have no faith?

4:41 And they feared exceedingly, and said one to another, What manner of man is this, that even the wind and the sea obey him?

5:1 And they came over unto the other side of the sea, into the country of the Gadarenes.

5:2 And when he was come out of the ship, immediately there met him out of the tombs a man with an unclean spirit,

5:3 Who had his dwelling among the tombs; and no man could bind him, no, not with chains:

5:4 Because that he had been often bound with fetters and chains, and the chains had been plucked asunder by him, and the fetters broken in pieces: neither could any man tame him.

5:5 And always, night and day, he was in the mountains, and in the tombs, crying, and cutting himself with stones.

5:6 But when he saw Jesus afar off, he ran and worshipped him,

5:7 And cried with a loud voice, and said, What have I to do with thee, Jesus, thou Son of the most high God? I adjure thee by God, that thou torment me not.

5:8 For he said unto him, Come out of the man, thou unclean spirit.

5:9 And he asked him, What is thy name? And he answered, saying, My name is Legion: for we are many.

5:10 And he besought him much that he would not send them away out of the country.

5:11 Now there was there nigh unto the mountains a great herd of swine feeding.

5:12 And all the devils besought him, saying, Send us into the swine, that we may enter into them.

5:13 And forthwith Jesus gave them leave. And the unclean spirits went out, and entered into the swine: and the herd ran violently down a steep place into the sea, (they were about two thousand;)

and were choked in the sea.

5:14 And they that fed the swine fled, and told it in the city, and in the country. And they went out to see what it was that was done.

5:15 And they come to Jesus, and see him that was possessed with the devil, and had the legion, sitting, and clothed, and in his right mind: and they were afraid.

5:16 And they that saw it told them how it befell to him that was possessed with the devil, and also concerning the swine.

5:17 And they began to pray him to depart out of their coasts.

5:18 And when he was come into the ship, he that had been possessed with the devil prayed him that he might be with him.

5:19 Howbeit Jesus suffered him not, but saith unto him, Go home to thy friends, and tell them how great things the Lord hath done for thee, and hath had compassion on thee.

5:20 And he departed, and began to publish in Decapolis how great things Jesus had done for him: and all men did marvel.

5:21 And when Jesus was passed over again by ship unto the other side, much people gathered unto him: and he was nigh unto the sea.

5:22 And, behold, there cometh one of the rulers of the synagogue, Jairus by name; and when he saw him, he fell at his feet,

5:23 And besought him greatly, saying, My little daughter lieth at the point of death: I pray thee, come and lay thy hands on her, that she may be healed; and she shall live.

5:24 And Jesus went with him; and much people followed him, and thronged him.

5:25 And a certain woman, which had an issue of blood twelve years, **5:26** And had suffered many things of many physicians, and had spent all that she had, and was nothing bettered, but rather grew worse, **5:27** When she had heard of Jesus, came in the press behind, and touched his garment.

5:28 For she said, If I may touch but his clothes, I shall be whole.

5:29 And straightway the fountain of her blood was dried up; and she felt in her body that she was healed of that plague.

5:30 And Jesus, immediately knowing in himself that virtue had gone out of him, turned him about in the press, and said, Who touched my clothes?

5:31 And his disciples said unto him, Thou seest the multitude thronging thee, and sayest thou, Who touched me?

5:32 And he looked round about to see her that had done this thing.

5:33 But the woman fearing and trembling, knowing what was done in her, came and fell down before him, and told him all the truth.

5:34 And he said unto her, Daughter, thy faith hath made thee whole; go in peace, and be whole of thy plague.

5:35 While he yet spake, there came from the ruler of the synagogue's house certain which said, Thy daughter is dead: why troublest thou the Master any further?

5:36 As soon as Jesus heard the word that was spoken, he saith unto the ruler of the synagogue, Be not afraid, only believe.

5:37 And he suffered no man to follow him, save Peter, and James, and John the brother of James.

5:38 And he cometh to the house of the ruler of the synagogue, and seeth the tumult, and them that wept and wailed greatly.

5:39 And when he was come in, he saith unto them, Why make ye this ado, and weep? the damsel is not dead, but sleepeth.

5:40 And they laughed him to scorn. But when he had put them all out, he taketh the father and the mother of the damsel, and them that were with him, and entereth in where the damsel was lying.

5:41 And he took the damsel by the hand, and said unto her, Talitha cumi; which is, being interpreted, Damsel, I say unto thee, arise.

5:42 And straightway the damsel arose, and walked; for she was of the age of twelve years. And they were astonished with a great astonishment.

5:43 And he charged them straitly that no man should know it; and commanded that something should be given her to eat.

6:1 And he went out from thence, and came into his own country; and his disciples follow him.

6:2 And when the sabbath day was come, he began to teach in the synagogue: and many hearing him were astonished, saying, From whence hath this man these things? and what wisdom is this which is given unto him, that even such mighty works are wrought by his hands?

6:3 Is not this the carpenter, the son of Mary, the brother of James, and Joses, and of Juda, and Simon? and are not his sisters here with us? And they were offended at him.

6:4 But Jesus, said unto them, A prophet is not without honour, but in his own country, and among his own kin, and in his own house.

6:5 And he could there do no mighty work, save that he laid his hands upon a few sick folk, and healed them.

6:6 And he marvelled because of their unbelief. And he went round about the villages, teaching.

6:7 And he called unto him the twelve, and began to send them forth by two and two; and gave them power over unclean spirits;

6:8 And commanded them that they should take nothing for their journey, save a staff only; no scrip, no bread, no money in their purse:

6:9 But be shod with sandals; and not put on two coats.

6:10 And he said unto them, In what place soever ye enter into an house, there abide till ye depart from that place.

6:11 And whosoever shall not receive you, nor hear you, when ye depart thence, shake off the dust under your feet for a testimony against them.

Verily I say unto you, It shall be more tolerable for Sodom and Gomorrha in the day of judgment, than for that city.

6:12 And they went out, and preached that men should repent.

6:13 And they cast out many devils, and anointed with oil many that were sick, and healed them.

6:14 And king Herod heard of him; (for his name was spread abroad:) and he said, That John the Baptist was risen from the dead, and therefore mighty works do shew forth themselves in him.

6:15 Others said, That it is Elias. And others said, That it is a prophet, or as one of the prophets.

6:16 But when Herod heard thereof, he said, It is John, whom I beheaded: he is risen from the dead.

6:17 For Herod himself had sent forth and laid hold upon John, and bound him in prison for Herodias' sake, his brother Philip's wife: for he had married her.

6:18 For John had said unto Herod, It is not lawful for thee to have thy brother's wife.

6:19 Therefore Herodias had a quarrel against him, and would have killed him; but she could not:

6:20 For Herod feared John, knowing that he was a just man and an holy, and observed him; and when he heard him, he did many things, and heard him gladly.

6:21 And when a convenient day was come, that Herod on his birthday made a supper to his lords, high captains, and chief estates of Galilee;

6:22 And when the daughter of the said Herodias came in, and danced, and pleased Herod and them that sat with him, the king said unto the damsel, Ask of me whatsoever thou wilt, and I will give it thee.

6:23 And he sware unto her, Whatsoever thou shalt ask of me, I will give it thee, unto the half of my kingdom.

6:24 And she went forth, and said unto her mother, What shall I ask? And she said, The head of John the Baptist.

6:25 And she came in straightway with haste unto the king, and asked, saying, I will that thou give me by and by in a charger the head of John the Baptist.

6:26 And the king was exceeding sorry; yet for his oath's sake, and for their sakes which sat with him, he would not reject her.

6:27 And immediately the king sent an executioner, and commanded his head to be brought: and he went and beheaded him in the prison, **6:28** And brought his head in a charger, and gave it to the damsel: and the damsel gave it to her mother.

6:29 And when his disciples heard of it, they came and took up his corpse, and laid it in a tomb.

6:30 And the apostles gathered themselves together unto Jesus, and told him all things, both what they had done, and what they had taught.

6:31 And he said unto them, Come ye yourselves apart into a desert place, and rest a while: for there were many coming and going, and they had no leisure so much as to eat.

6:32 And they departed into a desert place by ship privately.

6:33 And the people saw them departing, and many knew him, and ran afoot thither out of all cities, and outwent them, and came together unto him.

6:34 And Jesus, when he came out, saw much people, and was moved with compassion toward them, because they were as sheep not having a shepherd: and he began to teach them many things.

6:35 And when the day was now far spent, his disciples came unto him, and said, This is a desert place, and now the time is far passed:

6:36 Send them away, that they may go into the country round about, and into the villages, and buy themselves bread: for they have nothing to eat.

6:37 He answered and said unto them, Give ye them to eat. And they say unto him, Shall we go and buy two hundred pennyworth of bread, and give them to eat?

6:38 He saith unto them, How many loaves have ye? go and see. And when they knew, they say, Five, and two fishes.

6:39 And he commanded them to make all sit down by companies upon the green grass.

6:40 And they sat down in ranks, by hundreds, and by fifties.

6:41 And when he had taken the five loaves and the two fishes, he looked up to heaven, and blessed, and brake the loaves, and gave them to his disciples to set before them; and the two fishes divided he among them all.

6:42 And they did all eat, and were filled.

6:43 And they took up twelve baskets full of the fragments, and of the fishes.

6:44 And they that did eat of the loaves were about five thousand men.

6:45 And straightway he constrained his disciples to get into the ship, and to go to the other side before unto Bethsaida, while he sent away the people.

6:46 And when he had sent them away, he departed into a mountain to pray.

6:47 And when even was come, the ship was in the midst of the sea, and he alone on the land.

6:48 And he saw them toiling in rowing; for the wind was contrary unto them: and about the fourth watch of the night he cometh unto them, walking upon the sea, and would have passed by them.

6:49 But when they saw him walking upon the sea, they supposed it had been a spirit, and cried out:

6:50 For they all saw him, and were troubled. And immediately he talked with them, and saith unto them, Be of good cheer: it is I; be not afraid.

6:51 And he went up unto them into the ship; and the wind ceased: and they were sore amazed in themselves beyond measure, and wondered.

6:52 For they considered not the miracle of the loaves: for their heart was hardened.

6:53 And when they had passed over, they came into the land of Gennesaret, and drew to the shore.

6:54 And when they were come out of the ship, straightway they knew him,

6:55 And ran through that whole region round about, and began to carry about in beds those that were sick, where they heard he was.

6:56 And whithersoever he entered, into villages, or cities, or country, they laid the sick in the streets, and besought him that they might touch if it were but the border of his garment: and as many as touched him were made whole.

7:1 Then came together unto him the Pharisees, and certain of the scribes, which came from Jerusalem.

7:2 And when they saw some of his disciples eat bread with defiled, that is to say, with unwashen, hands, they found fault.

7:3 For the Pharisees, and all the Jews, except they wash their hands oft, eat not, holding the tradition of the elders.

7:4 And when they come from the market, except they wash, they eat not.

And many other things there be, which they have received to hold, as the washing of cups, and pots, brasen vessels, and of tables.

7:5 Then the Pharisees and scribes asked him, Why walk not thy disciples according to the tradition of the elders, but eat bread with unwashen hands?

7:6 He answered and said unto them, Well hath Esaias prophesied of you hypocrites, as it is written, This people honoureth me with their lips, but their heart is far from me.

7:7 Howbeit in vain do they worship me, teaching for doctrines the commandments of men.

7:8 For laying aside the commandment of God, ye hold the tradition of men, as the washing of pots and cups: and many other such like things ye do.

7:9 And he said unto them, Full well ye reject the commandment of God, that ye may keep your own tradition.

7:10 For Moses said, Honour thy father and thy mother; and, Whoso curseth father or mother, let him die the death:

7:11 But ye say, If a man shall say to his father or mother, It is Corban, that is to say, a gift, by whatsoever thou mightest be profited by me; he shall be free.

7:12 And ye suffer him no more to do ought for his father or his mother;

7:13 Making the word of God of none effect through your tradition, which ye have delivered: and many such like things do ye.

7:14 And when he had called all the people unto him, he said unto them, Hearken unto me every one of you, and understand:

7:15 There is nothing from without a man, that entering into him can defile him: but the things which come out of him, those are they that defile the man.

7:16 If any man have ears to hear, let him hear.

7:17 And when he was entered into the house from the people, his disciples asked him concerning the parable.

7:18 And he saith unto them, Are ye so without understanding also? Do ye not perceive, that whatsoever thing from without entereth into the man, it cannot defile him;

7:19 Because it entereth not into his heart, but into the belly, and goeth out into the draught, purging all meats?

7:20 And he said, That which cometh out of the man, that defileth the man.

7:21 For from within, out of the heart of men, proceed evil thoughts, adulteries, fornications, murders,

7:22 Thefts, covetousness, wickedness, deceit, lasciviousness, an evil eye, blasphemy, pride, foolishness:

7:23 All these evil things come from within, and defile the man.

7:24 And from thence he arose, and went into the borders of Tyre and Sidon, and entered into an house, and would have no man know it: but he could not be hid.

7:25 For a certain woman, whose young daughter had an unclean spirit, heard of him, and came and fell at his feet:

7:26 The woman was a Greek, a Syrophenician by nation; and she besought him that he would cast forth the devil out of her daughter.

7:27 But Jesus said unto her, Let the children first be filled: for it is not meet to take the children's bread, and to cast it unto the dogs.

7:28 And she answered and said unto him, Yes, Lord: yet the dogs under the table eat of the children's crumbs.

7:29 And he said unto her, For this saying go thy way; the devil is gone out of thy daughter.

7:30 And when she was come to her house, she found the devil gone out, and her daughter laid upon the bed.

7:31 And again, departing from the coasts of Tyre and Sidon, he came unto the sea of Galilee, through the midst of the coasts of Decapolis.

7:32 And they bring unto him one that was deaf, and had an impediment in his speech; and they beseech him to put his hand upon him.

7:33 And he took him aside from the multitude, and put his fingers into his ears, and he spit, and touched his tongue;

7:34 And looking up to heaven, he sighed, and saith unto him, Ephphatha, that is, Be opened.

7:35 And straightway his ears were opened, and the string of his tongue was loosed, and he spake plain.

7:36 And he charged them that they should tell no man: but the more he charged them, so much the more a great deal they published it; **7:37** And were beyond measure astonished, saying, He hath done all things well: he maketh both the deaf to hear, and the dumb to speak.

8:1 In those days the multitude being very great, and having nothing to eat, Jesus called his disciples unto him, and saith unto them,

8:2 I have compassion on the multitude, because they have now been with me three days, and have nothing to eat:

8:3 And if I send them away fasting to their own houses, they will faint by the way: for divers of them came from far.

8:4 And his disciples answered him, From whence can a man satisfy these men with bread here in the wilderness?

8:5 And he asked them, How many loaves have ye? And they said, Seven.

8:6 And he commanded the people to sit down on the ground: and he took the seven loaves, and gave thanks, and brake, and gave to his disciples to set before them; and they did set them before the people.

8:7 And they had a few small fishes: and he blessed, and commanded to set them also before them.

8:8 So they did eat, and were filled: and they took up of the broken meat that was left seven baskets.

8:9 And they that had eaten were about four thousand: and he sent them away.

8:10 And straightway he entered into a ship with his disciples, and came into the parts of Dalmanutha.

8:11 And the Pharisees came forth, and began to question with him, seeking of him a sign from heaven, tempting him.

8:12 And he sighed deeply in his spirit, and saith, Why doth this generation seek after a sign? verily I say unto you, There shall no sign be given unto this generation.

8:13 And he left them, and entering into the ship again departed to the other side.

8:14 Now the disciples had forgotten to take bread, neither had they in the ship with them more than one loaf.

8:15 And he charged them, saying, Take heed, beware of the leaven of the Pharisees, and of the leaven of Herod.

8:16 And they reasoned among themselves, saying, It is because we have no bread.

8:17 And when Jesus knew it, he saith unto them, Why reason ye, because ye have no bread? perceive ye not yet, neither understand? have ye your heart yet hardened?

8:18 Having eyes, see ye not? and having ears, hear ye not? and do ye not remember?

8:19 When I brake the five loaves among five thousand, how many baskets full of fragments took ye up? They say unto him, Twelve.

8:20 And when the seven among four thousand, how many baskets full of fragments took ye up? And they said, Seven.

8:21 And he said unto them, How is it that ye do not understand?

8:22 And he cometh to Bethsaida; and they bring a blind man unto him, and besought him to touch him.

8:23 And he took the blind man by the hand, and led him out of the town; and when he had spit on his eyes, and put his hands upon him, he asked him if he saw ought.

8:24 And he looked up, and said, I see men as trees, walking.

8:25 After that he put his hands again upon his eyes, and made him look up: and he was restored, and saw every man clearly.

8:26 And he sent him away to his house, saying, Neither go into the town, nor tell it to any in the town.

8:27 And Jesus went out, and his disciples, into the towns of Caesarea Philippi: and by the way he asked his disciples, saying unto them, Whom do men say that I am?

8:28 And they answered, John the Baptist; but some say, Elias; and others, One of the prophets.

8:29 And he saith unto them, But whom say ye that I am? And Peter answereth and saith unto him, Thou art the Christ.

8:30 And he charged them that they should tell no man of him.

8:31 And he began to teach them, that the Son of man must suffer many things, and be rejected of the elders, and of the chief priests, and scribes, and be killed, and after three days rise again.

8:32 And he spake that saying openly. And Peter took him, and began to rebuke him.

8:33 But when he had turned about and looked on his disciples, he rebuked Peter, saying, Get thee behind me, Satan: for thou savourest not the things that be of God, but the things that be of men.

8:34 And when he had called the people unto him with his disciples also, he said unto them, Whosoever will come after me, let him deny himself, and take up his cross, and follow me.

8:35 For whosoever will save his life shall lose it; but whosoever shall lose his life for my sake and the gospel's, the same shall save it.

8:36 For what shall it profit a man, if he shall gain the whole world, and lose his own soul?

8:37 Or what shall a man give in exchange for his soul?

8:38 Whosoever therefore shall be ashamed of me and of my words in this adulterous and sinful generation; of him also shall the Son of man be ashamed, when he cometh in the glory of his Father with the holy angels.

9:1 And he said unto them, Verily I say unto you, That there be some of them that stand here, which shall not taste of death, till they have seen the kingdom of God come with power.

9:2 And after six days Jesus taketh with him Peter, and James, and John, and leadeth them up into an high mountain apart by themselves: and he was transfigured before them.

9:3 And his raiment became shining, exceeding white as snow; so as no fuller on earth can white them.

9:4 And there appeared unto them Elias with Moses: and they were talking with Jesus.

9:5 And Peter answered and said to Jesus, Master, it is good for us to be here: and let us make three tabernacles; one for thee, and one for Moses, and one for Elias.

9:6 For he wist not what to say; for they were sore afraid.

9:7 And there was a cloud that overshadowed them: and a voice came out of the cloud, saying, This is my beloved Son: hear him.

9:8 And suddenly, when they had looked round about, they saw no man any more, save Jesus only with themselves.

9:9 And as they came down from the mountain, he charged them that they should tell no man what things they had seen, till the Son of man were risen from the dead.

9:10 And they kept that saying with themselves, questioning one with another what the rising from the dead should mean.

9:11 And they asked him, saying, Why say the scribes that Elias must first come?

9:12 And he answered and told them, Elias verily cometh first, and restoreth all things; and how it is written of the Son of man, that he must suffer many things, and be set at nought.

9:13 But I say unto you, That Elias is indeed come, and they have done unto him whatsoever they listed, as it is written of him.

9:14 And when he came to his disciples, he saw a great multitude about them, and the scribes questioning with them.

9:15 And straightway all the people, when they beheld him, were greatly amazed, and running to him saluted him.

9:16 And he asked the scribes, What question ye with them?

9:17 And one of the multitude answered and said, Master, I have brought unto thee my son, which hath a dumb spirit;

9:18 And wheresoever he taketh him, he teareth him: and he foameth, and gnasheth with his teeth, and pineth away: and I spake to thy disciples that they should cast him out; and they could not.

9:19 He answereth him, and saith, O faithless generation, how long shall I be with you? how long shall I suffer you? bring him unto me.

9:20 And they brought him unto him: and when he saw him, straightway the spirit tare him; and he fell on the ground, and wallowed foaming.

9:21 And he asked his father, How long is it ago since this came unto him? And he said, Of a child.

9:22 And ofttimes it hath cast him into the fire, and into the waters, to destroy him: but if thou canst do any thing, have compassion on us, and help us.

9:23 Jesus said unto him, If thou canst believe, all things are possible to him that believeth.

9:24 And straightway the father of the child cried out, and said with tears, Lord, I believe; help thou mine unbelief.

9:25 When Jesus saw that the people came running together, he rebuked the foul spirit, saying unto him, Thou dumb and deaf spirit, I charge thee, come out of him, and enter no more into him.

9:26 And the spirit cried, and rent him sore, and came out of him: and he was as one dead; insomuch that many said, He is dead.

9:27 But Jesus took him by the hand, and lifted him up; and he arose.

9:28 And when he was come into the house, his disciples asked him privately, Why could not we cast him out?

9:29 And he said unto them, This kind can come forth by nothing, but by prayer and fasting.

9:30 And they departed thence, and passed through Galilee; and he would not that any man should know it.

9:31 For he taught his disciples, and said unto them, The Son of man is delivered into the hands of men, and they shall kill him; and after that he is killed, he shall rise the third day.

9:32 But they understood not that saying, and were afraid to ask him.

9:33 And he came to Capernaum: and being in the house he asked them, What was it that ye disputed among yourselves by the way? **9:34** But they held their peace: for by the way they had disputed among themselves, who should be the greatest.

9:35 And he sat down, and called the twelve, and saith unto them, If any man desire to be first, the same shall be last of all, and servant of all.

9:36 And he took a child, and set him in the midst of them: and when he had taken him in his arms, he said unto them,

9:37 Whosoever shall receive one of such children in my name, receiveth me: and whosoever shall receive me, receiveth not me, but him that sent me.

9:38 And John answered him, saying, Master, we saw one casting out devils in thy name, and he followeth not us: and we forbad him, because he followeth not us.

9:39 But Jesus said, Forbid him not: for there is no man which shall do a miracle in my name, that can lightly speak evil of me.

9:40 For he that is not against us is on our part.

9:41 For whosoever shall give you a cup of water to drink in my name, because ye belong to Christ, verily I say unto you, he shall not lose his reward.

9:42 And whosoever shall offend one of these little ones that believe in me, it is better for him that a millstone were hanged about his neck, and he were cast into the sea.

9:43 And if thy hand offend thee, cut it off: it is better for thee to enter into life maimed, than having two hands to go into hell, into the fire that never shall be quenched:

9:44 Where their worm dieth not, and the fire is not quenched.

9:45 And if thy foot offend thee, cut it off: it is better for thee to enter halt into life, than having two feet to be cast into hell, into the fire that never shall be quenched:

9:46 Where their worm dieth not, and the fire is not quenched.

9:47 And if thine eye offend thee, pluck it out: it is better for thee to enter into the kingdom of God with one eye, than having two eyes to be cast into hell fire:

9:48 Where their worm dieth not, and the fire is not quenched.

9:49 For every one shall be salted with fire, and every sacrifice shall be salted with salt.

9:50 Salt is good: but if the salt have lost his saltness, wherewith will ye season it? Have salt in yourselves, and have peace one with another.

10:1 And he arose from thence, and cometh into the coasts of Judaea by the farther side of Jordan: and the people resort unto him again; and, as he was wont, he taught them again.

10:2 And the Pharisees came to him, and asked him, Is it lawful for a man to put away his wife? tempting him.

10:3 And he answered and said unto them, What did Moses command you?

10:4 And they said, Moses suffered to write a bill of divorcement, and to put her away.

10:5 And Jesus answered and said unto them, For the hardness of your heart he wrote you this precept.

10:6 But from the beginning of the creation God made them male and female.

10:7 For this cause shall a man leave his father and mother, and cleave to his wife;

10:8 And they twain shall be one flesh: so then they are no more twain, but one flesh.

10:9 What therefore God hath joined together, let not man put asunder.

10:10 And in the house his disciples asked him again of the same matter.

10:11 And he saith unto them, Whosoever shall put away his wife, and marry another, committeth adultery against her.

10:12 And if a woman shall put away her husband, and be married to another, she committeth adultery.

10:13 And they brought young children to him, that he should touch them: and his disciples rebuked those that brought them.

10:14 But when Jesus saw it, he was much displeased, and said unto them, Suffer the little children to come unto me, and forbid them not: for of such is the kingdom of God.

10:15 Verily I say unto you, Whosoever shall not receive the kingdom of God as a little child, he shall not enter therein.

10:16 And he took them up in his arms, put his hands upon them, and blessed them.

10:17 And when he was gone forth into the way, there came one running, and kneeled to him, and asked him, Good Master, what shall I do that I may inherit eternal life?

10:18 And Jesus said unto him, Why callest thou me good? there is none good but one, that is, God.

10:19 Thou knowest the commandments, Do not commit adultery, Do not kill, Do not steal, Do not bear false witness, Defraud not, Honour thy father and mother.

10:20 And he answered and said unto him, Master, all these have I observed from my youth.

10:21 Then Jesus beholding him loved him, and said unto him, One thing thou lackest: go thy way, sell whatsoever thou hast, and give to the poor, and thou shalt have treasure in heaven: and come, take up the cross, and follow me.

10:22 And he was sad at that saying, and went away grieved: for he had great possessions.

10:23 And Jesus looked round about, and saith unto his disciples, How hardly shall they that have riches enter into the kingdom of God! **10:24** And the disciples were astonished at his words. But Jesus answereth again, and saith unto them, Children, how hard is it for them that trust in riches to enter into the kingdom of God!

10:25 It is easier for a camel to go through the eye of a needle, than for a rich man to enter into the kingdom of God.

10:26 And they were astonished out of measure, saying among themselves, Who then can be saved?

10:27 And Jesus looking upon them saith, With men it is impossible, but not with God: for with God all things are possible.

10:28 Then Peter began to say unto him, Lo, we have left all, and have followed thee.

10:29 And Jesus answered and said, Verily I say unto you, There is no man that hath left house, or brethren, or sisters, or father, or mother, or wife, or children, or lands, for my sake, and the gospel's,

10:30 But he shall receive an hundredfold now in this time, houses, and brethren, and sisters, and mothers, and children, and lands, with persecutions; and in the world to come eternal life.

10:31 But many that are first shall be last; and the last first.

10:32 And they were in the way going up to Jerusalem; and Jesus went before them: and they were amazed; and as they followed, they were afraid.

And he took again the twelve, and began to tell them what things should happen unto him,

10:33 Saying, Behold, we go up to Jerusalem; and the Son of man shall be delivered unto the chief priests, and unto the scribes; and they shall condemn him to death, and shall deliver him to the Gentiles:

10:34 And they shall mock him, and shall scourge him, and shall spit upon him, and shall kill him: and the third day he shall rise again.

10:35 And James and John, the sons of Zebedee, come unto him, saying, Master, we would that thou shouldest do for us whatsoever we shall desire.

10:36 And he said unto them, What would ye that I should do for you?

10:37 They said unto him, Grant unto us that we may sit, one on thy right hand, and the other on thy left hand, in thy glory.

10:38 But Jesus said unto them, Ye know not what ye ask: can ye drink of the cup that I drink of? and be baptized with the baptism that I am baptized with?

10:39 And they said unto him, We can. And Jesus said unto them, Ye shall indeed drink of the cup that I drink of; and with the baptism that I am baptized withal shall ye be baptized:

10:40 But to sit on my right hand and on my left hand is not mine to give; but it shall be given to them for whom it is prepared.

10:41 And when the ten heard it, they began to be much displeased with James and John.

10:42 But Jesus called them to him, and saith unto them, Ye know that they which are accounted to rule over the Gentiles exercise lordship over them; and their great ones exercise authority upon them.

10:43 But so shall it not be among you: but whosoever will be great among you, shall be your minister:

10:44 And whosoever of you will be the chiefest, shall be servant of all.

10:45 For even the Son of man came not to be ministered unto, but to minister, and to give his life a ransom for many.

10:46 And they came to Jericho: and as he went out of Jericho with his disciples and a great number of people, blind Bartimaeus, the son of Timaeus, sat by the highway side begging.

10:47 And when he heard that it was Jesus of Nazareth, he began to cry out, and say, Jesus, thou son of David, have mercy on me.

10:48 And many charged him that he should hold his peace: but he cried the more a great deal, Thou son of David, have mercy on me.

10:49 And Jesus stood still, and commanded him to be called. And they call the blind man, saying unto him, Be of good comfort, rise; he calleth thee.

10:50 And he, casting away his garment, rose, and came to Jesus.

10:51 And Jesus answered and said unto him, What wilt thou that I should do unto thee? The blind man said unto him, Lord, that I might receive my sight.

10:52 And Jesus said unto him, Go thy way; thy faith hath made thee whole.

And immediately he received his sight, and followed Jesus in the way.

11:1 And when they came nigh to Jerusalem, unto Bethphage and Bethany, at the mount of Olives, he sendeth forth two of his disciples, **11:2** And saith unto them, Go your way into the village over against you: and as soon as ye be entered into it, ye shall find a colt tied, whereon never man sat; loose him, and bring him.

11:3 And if any man say unto you, Why do ye this? say ye that the Lord hath need of him; and straightway he will send him hither.

11:4 And they went their way, and found the colt tied by the door without in a place where two ways met; and they loose him.

11:5 And certain of them that stood there said unto them, What do ye, loosing the colt?

11:6 And they said unto them even as Jesus had commanded: and they let them go.

11:7 And they brought the colt to Jesus, and cast their garments on him; and he sat upon him.

11:8 And many spread their garments in the way: and others cut down branches off the trees, and strawed them in the way.

11:9 And they that went before, and they that followed, cried, saying, Hosanna; Blessed is he that cometh in the name of the Lord:

11:10 Blessed be the kingdom of our father David, that cometh in the name of the Lord: Hosanna in the highest.

11:11 And Jesus entered into Jerusalem, and into the temple: and when he had looked round about upon all things, and now the eventide was come, he went out unto Bethany with the twelve.

11:12 And on the morrow, when they were come from Bethany, he was hungry:

11:13 And seeing a fig tree afar off having leaves, he came, if haply he might find any thing thereon: and when he came to it, he found nothing but leaves; for the time of figs was not yet.

11:14 And Jesus answered and said unto it, No man eat fruit of thee hereafter for ever. And his disciples heard it.

11:15 And they come to Jerusalem: and Jesus went into the temple, and began to cast out them that sold and bought in the temple, and overthrew the tables of the moneychangers, and the seats of them that sold doves;

11:16 And would not suffer that any man should carry any vessel through the temple.

11:17 And he taught, saying unto them, Is it not written, My house shall be called of all nations the house of prayer? but ye have made it a den of thieves.

11:18 And the scribes and chief priests heard it, and sought how they might destroy him: for they feared him, because all the people was astonished at his doctrine.

11:19 And when even was come, he went out of the city.

11:20 And in the morning, as they passed by, they saw the fig tree dried up from the roots.

11:21 And Peter calling to remembrance saith unto him, Master, behold, the fig tree which thou cursedst is withered away.

11:22 And Jesus answering saith unto them, Have faith in God.

11:23 For verily I say unto you, That whosoever shall say unto this mountain, Be thou removed, and be thou cast into the sea; and shall not doubt in his heart, but shall believe that those things which he saith shall come to pass; he shall have whatsoever he saith.

11:24 Therefore I say unto you, What things soever ye desire, when ye pray, believe that ye receive them, and ye shall have them.

11:25 And when ye stand praying, forgive, if ye have ought against any: that your Father also which is in heaven may forgive you your trespasses.

11:26 But if ye do not forgive, neither will your Father which is in heaven forgive your trespasses.

11:27 And they come again to Jerusalem: and as he was walking in the temple, there come to him the chief priests, and the scribes, and the elders,

11:28 And say unto him, By what authority doest thou these things? and who gave thee this authority to do these things?

11:29 And Jesus answered and said unto them, I will also ask of you one question, and answer me, and I will tell you by what authority I do these things.

11:30 The baptism of John, was it from heaven, or of men? answer me.

11:31 And they reasoned with themselves, saying, If we shall say, From heaven; he will say, Why then did ye not believe him?

11:32 But if we shall say, Of men; they feared the people: for all men counted John, that he was a prophet indeed.

11:33 And they answered and said unto Jesus, We cannot tell. And Jesus answering saith unto them, Neither do I tell you by what authority I do these things.

12:1 And he began to speak unto them by parables. A certain man planted a vineyard, and set an hedge about it, and digged a place for the winefat, and built a tower, and let it out to husbandmen, and went into a far country.

12:2 And at the season he sent to the husbandmen a servant, that he might receive from the husbandmen of the fruit of the vineyard.

12:3 And they caught him, and beat him, and sent him away empty.

12:4 And again he sent unto them another servant; and at him they cast stones, and wounded him in the head, and sent him away shamefully handled.

12:5 And again he sent another; and him they killed, and many others; beating some, and killing some.

12:6 Having yet therefore one son, his wellbeloved, he sent him also last unto them, saying, They will reverence my son.

12:7 But those husbandmen said among themselves, This is the heir; come, let us kill him, and the inheritance shall be our's.

12:8 And they took him, and killed him, and cast him out of the vineyard.

12:9 What shall therefore the lord of the vineyard do? he will come and destroy the husbandmen, and will give the vineyard unto others.

12:10 And have ye not read this scripture; The stone which the builders rejected is become the head of the corner:

12:11 This was the Lord's doing, and it is marvellous in our eyes?
12:12 And they sought to lay hold on him, but feared the people: for they knew that he had spoken the parable against them: and they left him, and went their way.

12:13 And they send unto him certain of the Pharisees and of the Herodians, to catch him in his words.

12:14 And when they were come, they say unto him, Master, we know that thou art true, and carest for no man: for thou regardest not the person of men, but teachest the way of God in truth: Is it lawful to give tribute to Caesar, or not?

12:15 Shall we give, or shall we not give? But he, knowing their hypocrisy, said unto them, Why tempt ye me? bring me a penny, that I may see it.

12:16 And they brought it. And he saith unto them, Whose is this image and superscription? And they said unto him, Caesar's.

12:17 And Jesus answering said unto them, Render to Caesar the things that are Caesar's, and to God the things that are God's. And they marvelled at him.

12:18 Then come unto him the Sadducees, which say there is no resurrection; and they asked him, saying,

12:19 Master, Moses wrote unto us, If a man's brother die, and leave his wife behind him, and leave no children, that his brother should take his wife, and raise up seed unto his brother.

12:20 Now there were seven brethren: and the first took a wife, and dying left no seed.

12:21 And the second took her, and died, neither left he any seed: and the third likewise.

12:22 And the seven had her, and left no seed: last of all the woman died also.

12:23 In the resurrection therefore, when they shall rise, whose wife shall she be of them? for the seven had her to wife.

12:24 And Jesus answering said unto them, Do ye not therefore err, because ye know not the scriptures, neither the power of God?

12:25 For when they shall rise from the dead, they neither marry, nor are given in marriage; but are as the angels which are in heaven.

12:26 And as touching the dead, that they rise: have ye not read in the book of Moses, how in the bush God spake unto him, saying, I am the God of Abraham, and the God of Isaac, and the God of Jacob? **12:27** He is not the God of the dead, but the God of the living: ye therefore do greatly err.

12:28 And one of the scribes came, and having heard them reasoning together, and perceiving that he had answered them well, asked him, Which is the first commandment of all?

12:29 And Jesus answered him, The first of all the commandments is, Hear, O Israel; The Lord our God is one Lord:

12:30 And thou shalt love the Lord thy God with all thy heart, and with all thy soul, and with all thy mind, and with all thy strength: this is the first commandment.

12:31 And the second is like, namely this, Thou shalt love thy neighbour as thyself. There is none other commandment greater than these.

12:32 And the scribe said unto him, Well, Master, thou hast said the truth: for there is one God; and there is none other but he:

12:33 And to love him with all the heart, and with all the understanding, and with all the soul, and with all the strength, and to love his neighbour as himself, is more than all whole burnt offerings and sacrifices.

12:34 And when Jesus saw that he answered discreetly, he said unto him, Thou art not far from the kingdom of God. And no man after that durst ask him any question.

12:35 And Jesus answered and said, while he taught in the temple,

How say the scribes that Christ is the son of David?

12:36 For David himself said by the Holy Ghost, The LORD said to my Lord, Sit thou on my right hand, till I make thine enemies thy footstool.

12:37 David therefore himself calleth him Lord; and whence is he then his son? And the common people heard him gladly.

12:38 And he said unto them in his doctrine, Beware of the scribes, which love to go in long clothing, and love salutations in the marketplaces,

12:39 And the chief seats in the synagogues, and the uppermost rooms at feasts:

12:40 Which devour widows' houses, and for a pretence make long prayers: these shall receive greater damnation.

12:41 And Jesus sat over against the treasury, and beheld how the people cast money into the treasury: and many that were rich cast in much.

12:42 And there came a certain poor widow, and she threw in two mites, which make a farthing.

12:43 And he called unto him his disciples, and saith unto them, Verily I say unto you, That this poor widow hath cast more in, than all they which have cast into the treasury:

12:44 For all they did cast in of their abundance; but she of her want did cast in all that she had, even all her living.

13:1 And as he went out of the temple, one of his disciples saith unto him, Master, see what manner of stones and what buildings are here! **13:2** And Jesus answering said unto him, Seest thou these great buildings? there shall not be left one stone upon another, that shall not be thrown down.

13:3 And as he sat upon the mount of Olives over against the temple, Peter and James and John and Andrew asked him privately,

13:4 Tell us, when shall these things be? and what shall be the sign when all these things shall be fulfilled?

13:5 And Jesus answering them began to say, Take heed lest any man deceive you:

13:6 For many shall come in my name, saying, I am Christ; and shall deceive many.

13:7 And when ye shall hear of wars and rumours of wars, be ye not troubled: for such things must needs be; but the end shall not be yet.

13:8 For nation shall rise against nation, and kingdom against kingdom: and there shall be earthquakes in divers places, and there shall be famines and troubles: these are the beginnings of sorrows.

13:9 But take heed to yourselves: for they shall deliver you up to councils; and in the synagogues ye shall be beaten: and ye shall be brought before rulers and kings for my sake, for a testimony against them.

13:10 And the gospel must first be published among all nations.

13:11 But when they shall lead you, and deliver you up, take no thought beforehand what ye shall speak, neither do ye premeditate: but whatsoever shall be given you in that hour, that speak ye: for it is not ye that speak, but the Holy Ghost.

13:12 Now the brother shall betray the brother to death, and the father the son; and children shall rise up against their parents, and shall cause them to be put to death.

13:13 And ye shall be hated of all men for my name's sake: but he that shall endure unto the end, the same shall be saved.

13:14 But when ye shall see the abomination of desolation, spoken of by Daniel the prophet, standing where it ought not, (let him that readeth understand,) then let them that be in Judaea flee to the mountains:

13:15 And let him that is on the housetop not go down into the house, neither enter therein, to take any thing out of his house:

13:16 And let him that is in the field not turn back again for to take up his garment.

13:17 But woe to them that are with child, and to them that give suck in those days!

13:18 And pray ye that your flight be not in the winter.

13:19 For in those days shall be affliction, such as was not from the beginning of the creation which God created unto this time, neither shall be.

13:20 And except that the Lord had shortened those days, no flesh should be saved: but for the elect's sake, whom he hath chosen, he hath shortened the days.

13:21 And then if any man shall say to you, Lo, here is Christ; or, lo, he is there; believe him not:

13:22 For false Christs and false prophets shall rise, and shall shew signs and wonders, to seduce, if it were possible, even the elect.

13:23 But take ye heed: behold, I have foretold you all things.

13:24 But in those days, after that tribulation, the sun shall be darkened, and the moon shall not give her light,

13:25 And the stars of heaven shall fall, and the powers that are in heaven shall be shaken.

13:26 And then shall they see the Son of man coming in the clouds with great power and glory.

13:27 And then shall he send his angels, and shall gather together his elect from the four winds, from the uttermost part of the earth to the uttermost part of heaven.

13:28 Now learn a parable of the fig tree; When her branch is yet tender, and putteth forth leaves, ye know that summer is near:

13:29 So ye in like manner, when ye shall see these things come to pass, know that it is nigh, even at the doors.

13:30 Verily I say unto you, that this generation shall not pass, till all these things be done.

13:31 Heaven and earth shall pass away: but my words shall not pass away.

13:32 But of that day and that hour knoweth no man, no, not the angels which are in heaven, neither the Son, but the Father.

13:33 Take ye heed, watch and pray: for ye know not when the time is.

13:34 For the Son of Man is as a man taking a far journey, who left his house, and gave authority to his servants, and to every man his work, and commanded the porter to watch.

13:35 Watch ye therefore: for ye know not when the master of the house cometh, at even, or at midnight, or at the cockcrowing, or in the morning:

13:36 Lest coming suddenly he find you sleeping.

13:37 And what I say unto you I say unto all, Watch.

14:1 After two days was the feast of the passover, and of unleavened bread: and the chief priests and the scribes sought how they might take him by craft, and put him to death.

14:2 But they said, Not on the feast day, lest there be an uproar of the people.

14:3 And being in Bethany in the house of Simon the leper, as he sat at meat, there came a woman having an alabaster box of ointment of spikenard very precious; and she brake the box, and poured it on his head.

14:4 And there were some that had indignation within themselves, and said, Why was this waste of the ointment made?

14:5 For it might have been sold for more than three hundred pence, and have been given to the poor. And they murmured against her.

14:6 And Jesus said, Let her alone; why trouble ye her? she hath wrought a good work on me.

14:7 For ye have the poor with you always, and whensoever ye will ye may do them good: but me ye have not always.

14:8 She hath done what she could: she is come aforehand to anoint my body to the burying.

14:9 Verily I say unto you, Wheresoever this gospel shall be preached throughout the whole world, this also that she hath done shall be spoken of for a memorial of her.

14:10 And Judas Iscariot, one of the twelve, went unto the chief priests, to betray him unto them.

14:11 And when they heard it, they were glad, and promised to give him money. And he sought how he might conveniently betray him.

14:12 And the first day of unleavened bread, when they killed the passover, his disciples said unto him, Where wilt thou that we go and prepare that thou mayest eat the passover?

14:13 And he sendeth forth two of his disciples, and saith unto them, Go ye into the city, and there shall meet you a man bearing a pitcher of water: follow him.

14:14 And wheresoever he shall go in, say ye to the goodman of the house, The Master saith, Where is the guestchamber, where I shall eat the passover with my disciples?

14:15 And he will shew you a large upper room furnished and prepared: there make ready for us.

14:16 And his disciples went forth, and came into the city, and found as he had said unto them: and they made ready the passover.

14:17 And in the evening he cometh with the twelve.

14:18 And as they sat and did eat, Jesus said, Verily I say unto you, One of you which eateth with me shall betray me.

14:19 And they began to be sorrowful, and to say unto him one by one, Is it I? and another said, Is it I?

14:20 And he answered and said unto them, It is one of the twelve, that dippeth with me in the dish.

14:21 The Son of man indeed goeth, as it is written of him: but woe to that man by whom the Son of man is betrayed! good were it for that man if he had never been born.

14:22 And as they did eat, Jesus took bread, and blessed, and brake it, and gave to them, and said, Take, eat: this is my body.

14:23 And he took the cup, and when he had given thanks, he gave it to them: and they all drank of it.

14:24 And he said unto them, This is my blood of the new testament, which is shed for many.

14:25 Verily I say unto you, I will drink no more of the fruit of the vine, until that day that I drink it new in the kingdom of God.

14:26 And when they had sung an hymn, they went out into the mount of Olives.

14:27 And Jesus saith unto them, All ye shall be offended because of me this night: for it is written, I will smite the shepherd, and the sheep shall be scattered.

14:28 But after that I am risen, I will go before you into Galilee.

14:29 But Peter said unto him, Although all shall be offended, yet will not I.

14:30 And Jesus saith unto him, Verily I say unto thee, That this day, even in this night, before the cock crow twice, thou shalt deny me thrice.

14:31 But he spake the more vehemently, If I should die with thee, I will not deny thee in any wise. Likewise also said they all.

14:32 And they came to a place which was named Gethsemane: and he saith to his disciples, Sit ye here, while I shall pray.

14:33 And he taketh with him Peter and James and John, and began to be sore amazed, and to be very heavy;

14:34 And saith unto them, My soul is exceeding sorrowful unto death: tarry ye here, and watch.

14:35 And he went forward a little, and fell on the ground, and prayed that, if it were possible, the hour might pass from him.

14:36 And he said, Abba, Father, all things are possible unto thee; take away this cup from me: nevertheless not what I will, but what thou wilt.

14:37 And he cometh, and findeth them sleeping, and saith unto Peter, Simon, sleepest thou? couldest not thou watch one hour?

14:38 Watch ye and pray, lest ye enter into temptation. The spirit truly is ready, but the flesh is weak.

14:39 And again he went away, and prayed, and spake the same words.

14:40 And when he returned, he found them asleep again, (for their eyes were heavy,) neither wist they what to answer him.

14:41 And he cometh the third time, and saith unto them, Sleep on now, and take your rest: it is enough, the hour is come; behold, the Son of man is betrayed into the hands of sinners.

14:42 Rise up, let us go; lo, he that betrayeth me is at hand.

14:43 And immediately, while he yet spake, cometh Judas, one of the twelve, and with him a great multitude with swords and staves, from the chief priests and the scribes and the elders.

14:44 And he that betrayed him had given them a token, saying, Whomsoever I shall kiss, that same is he; take him, and lead him away safely.

14:45 And as soon as he was come, he goeth straightway to him, and saith, Master, master; and kissed him.

14:46 And they laid their hands on him, and took him.

14:47 And one of them that stood by drew a sword, and smote a servant of the high priest, and cut off his ear.

14:48 And Jesus answered and said unto them, Are ye come out, as against a thief, with swords and with staves to take me?

14:49 I was daily with you in the temple teaching, and ye took me not: but the scriptures must be fulfilled.

14:50 And they all forsook him, and fled.

14:51 And there followed him a certain young man, having a linen cloth cast about his naked body; and the young men laid hold on him: **14:52** And he left the linen cloth, and fled from them naked.

14:53 And they led Jesus away to the high priest: and with him were assembled all the chief priests and the elders and the scribes.

14:54 And Peter followed him afar off, even into the palace of the high priest: and he sat with the servants, and warmed himself at the fire.

14:55 And the chief priests and all the council sought for witness against Jesus to put him to death; and found none.

14:56 For many bare false witness against him, but their witness agreed not together.

14:57 And there arose certain, and bare false witness against him, saying,

14:58 We heard him say, I will destroy this temple that is made with hands, and within three days I will build another made without hands.

14:59 But neither so did their witness agree together.

14:60 And the high priest stood up in the midst, and asked Jesus, saying, Answerest thou nothing? what is it which these witness against thee?

14:61 But he held his peace, and answered nothing. Again the high priest asked him, and said unto him, Art thou the Christ, the Son of the Blessed?

14:62 And Jesus said, I am: and ye shall see the Son of man sitting on the right hand of power, and coming in the clouds of heaven.

14:63 Then the high priest rent his clothes, and saith, What need we any further witnesses?

14:64 Ye have heard the blasphemy: what think ye? And they all condemned him to be guilty of death.

14:65 And some began to spit on him, and to cover his face, and to buffet him, and to say unto him, Prophesy: and the servants did strike him with the palms of their hands.

14:66 And as Peter was beneath in the palace, there cometh one of the maids of the high priest:

14:67 And when she saw Peter warming himself, she looked upon him, and said, And thou also wast with Jesus of Nazareth.

14:68 But he denied, saying, I know not, neither understand I what thou sayest. And he went out into the porch; and the cock crew.

14:69 And a maid saw him again, and began to say to them that stood by, This is one of them.

14:70 And he denied it again. And a little after, they that stood by said again to Peter, Surely thou art one of them: for thou art a Galilaean, and thy speech agreeth thereto.

14:71 But he began to curse and to swear, saying, I know not this man of whom ye speak.

14:72 And the second time the cock crew. And Peter called to mind the word that Jesus said unto him, Before the cock crow twice, thou shalt deny me thrice. And when he thought thereon, he wept.

15:1 And straightway in the morning the chief priests held a consultation with the elders and scribes and the whole council, and bound Jesus, and carried him away, and delivered him to Pilate.

15:2 And Pilate asked him, Art thou the King of the Jews? And he answering said unto them, Thou sayest it.

15:3 And the chief priests accused him of many things: but he answered nothing.

15:4 And Pilate asked him again, saying, Answerest thou nothing? behold how many things they witness against thee.

15:5 But Jesus yet answered nothing; so that Pilate marvelled.

15:6 Now at that feast he released unto them one prisoner, whomsoever they desired.

15:7 And there was one named Barabbas, which lay bound with them that had made insurrection with him, who had committed murder in the insurrection.

15:8 And the multitude crying aloud began to desire him to do as he had ever done unto them.

15:9 But Pilate answered them, saying, Will ye that I release unto you the King of the Jews?

15:10 For he knew that the chief priests had delivered him for envy.

15:11 But the chief priests moved the people, that he should rather release Barabbas unto them.

15:12 And Pilate answered and said again unto them, What will ye then that I shall do unto him whom ye call the King of the Jews? **15:13** And they cried out again, Crucify him.

15:14 Then Pilate said unto them, Why, what evil hath he done?

And they cried out the more exceedingly, Crucify him.

15:15 And so Pilate, willing to content the people, released Barabbas unto them, and delivered Jesus, when he had scourged him, to be crucified.

15:16 And the soldiers led him away into the hall, called Praetorium; and they call together the whole band.

15:17 And they clothed him with purple, and platted a crown of thorns, and put it about his head,

15:18 And began to salute him, Hail, King of the Jews!

15:19 And they smote him on the head with a reed, and did spit upon him, and bowing their knees worshipped him.

15:20 And when they had mocked him, they took off the purple from him, and put his own clothes on him, and led him out to crucify him.

15:21 And they compel one Simon a Cyrenian, who passed by, coming out of the country, the father of Alexander and Rufus, to bear his cross.

15:22 And they bring him unto the place Golgotha, which is, being interpreted, The place of a skull.

15:23 And they gave him to drink wine mingled with myrrh: but he received it not.

15:24 And when they had crucified him, they parted his garments, casting lots upon them, what every man should take.

15:25 And it was the third hour, and they crucified him.

15:26 And the superscription of his accusation was written over, THE KING OF THE JEWS.

15:27 And with him they crucify two thieves; the one on his right hand, and the other on his left.

15:28 And the scripture was fulfilled, which saith, And he was numbered with the transgressors.

15:29 And they that passed by railed on him, wagging their heads, and saying, Ah, thou that destroyest the temple, and buildest it in three days,

15:30 Save thyself, and come down from the cross.

15:31 Likewise also the chief priests mocking said among themselves with the scribes, He saved others; himself he cannot save.

15:32 Let Christ the King of Israel descend now from the cross, that we may see and believe. And they that were crucified with him reviled him.

15:33 And when the sixth hour was come, there was darkness over the whole land until the ninth hour.

15:34 And at the ninth hour Jesus cried with a loud voice, saying, Eloi, Eloi, lama sabachthani? which is, being interpreted, My God, my God, why hast thou forsaken me?

15:35 And some of them that stood by, when they heard it, said, Behold, he calleth Elias.

15:36 And one ran and filled a spunge full of vinegar, and put it on a reed, and gave him to drink, saying, Let alone; let us see whether Elias will come to take him down.

15:37 And Jesus cried with a loud voice, and gave up the ghost.

15:38 And the veil of the temple was rent in twain from the top to the bottom.

15:39 And when the centurion, which stood over against him, saw that he so cried out, and gave up the ghost, he said, Truly this man was the Son of God.

15:40 There were also women looking on afar off: among whom was Mary Magdalene, and Mary the mother of James the less and of Joses, and Salome;

15:41 (Who also, when he was in Galilee, followed him, and ministered unto him;) and many other women which came up with him unto Jerusalem.

15:42 And now when the even was come, because it was the preparation, that is, the day before the sabbath,

15:43 Joseph of Arimathaea, an honourable counsellor, which also waited for the kingdom of God, came, and went in boldly unto Pilate, and craved the body of Jesus.

15:44 And Pilate marvelled if he were already dead: and calling unto him the centurion, he asked him whether he had been any while dead.

15:45 And when he knew it of the centurion, he gave the body to Joseph.

15:46 And he bought fine linen, and took him down, and wrapped him in the linen, and laid him in a sepulchre which was hewn out of a rock, and rolled a stone unto the door of the sepulchre.

15:47 And Mary Magdalene and Mary the mother of Joses beheld where he was laid.

16:1 And when the sabbath was past, Mary Magdalene, and Mary the mother of James, and Salome, had bought sweet spices, that they might come and anoint him.

16:2 And very early in the morning the first day of the week, they came unto the sepulchre at the rising of the sun.

16:3 And they said among themselves, Who shall roll us away the stone from the door of the sepulchre?

16:4 And when they looked, they saw that the stone was rolled away: for it was very great.

16:5 And entering into the sepulchre, they saw a young man sitting on the right side, clothed in a long white garment; and they were affrighted.

16:6 And he saith unto them, Be not affrighted: Ye seek Jesus of Nazareth, which was crucified: he is risen; he is not here: behold the place where they laid him.

16:7 But go your way, tell his disciples and Peter that he goeth before you into Galilee: there shall ye see him, as he said unto you.

16:8 And they went out quickly, and fled from the sepulchre; for they trembled and were amazed: neither said they any thing to any man; for they were afraid.

16:9 Now when Jesus was risen early the first day of the week, he appeared first to Mary Magdalene, out of whom he had cast seven devils.

16:10 And she went and told them that had been with him, as they mourned and wept.

16:11 And they, when they had heard that he was alive, and had been seen of her, believed not.

16:12 After that he appeared in another form unto two of them, as they walked, and went into the country.

16:13 And they went and told it unto the residue: neither believed they them.

16:14 Afterward he appeared unto the eleven as they sat at meat, and upbraided them with their unbelief and hardness of heart, because they believed not them which had seen him after he was risen.

16:16 He that believeth and is baptized shall be saved; but he that believeth not shall be damned.

16:17 And these signs shall follow them that believe; In my name shall they cast out devils; they shall speak with new tongues;

16:18 They shall take up serpents; and if they drink any deadly thing, it shall not hurt them; they shall lay hands on the sick, and they shall recover.

16:19 So then after the Lord had spoken unto them, he was received up into heaven, and sat on the right hand of God.

16:20 And they went forth, and preached every where, the Lord working with them, and confirming the word with signs following. Amen.

God and email.

Made in the USA
Monee, IL
07 July 2026

56550159R00089